THE TECHNOLOGY FACADE

Overcoming Barriers to Effective Instructional Technology

LAWRENCE A. TOMEI

Duquesne University

ALLYN AND BACON

Boston ■ London ■ Toronto ■ Sydney ■ Tokyo ■ Singapore

Series Editor: Arnis E. Burvikovs
Editorial Assistant: Matthew Forster
Marketing Manager: Amy Cronin
Editorial-Production Service: Omegatype Typography, Inc.
Composition and Prepress Buyer: Linda Cox
Manufacturing Buyer: Julie McNeill
Cover Administrator: Kristina Mose-Libon
Electronic Composition: Omegatype Typography, Inc.

Library of Congress Cataloging-in-Publication Data

Tomei, Lawrence A.
    The technology facade : overcoming barriers to effective instructional technology / Lawrence A. Tomei.
        p.   cm.
    Includes bibliographical references and index.
    ISBN 0-205-32676-5 (alk. paper)
    1. Educational technology—United States.   2. Educational technology—United States—Finance.   3. Educational innovations—United States.   I. Title.

LB1028.3 .T66 2002
371.33—dc21

                                                                                    2001046384

Printed in the United States of America
10 9 8 7 6 5 4 3 2   06 05 04 03

This book is dedicated to my family . . .

To my wife, who was the first teacher to make me want to become an educator. To my daughters, who continue to teach me the only truly important things in life. To my brother and sister and their families, who remind me every day what it means to be a family. And to my Dad, my most ardent fan, who lost his wife of 55 years and our mother during the preparation of this book. Together, this small group of individuals has affected my life in more ways than they can ever imagine.

CONTENTS

PART V   EPILOGUE   205

PREFACE

■ ■ ■ ■ ■

INTRODUCING THE TECHNOLOGY FACADE

Schools are spending money for technology at an alarming rate. Of the more than $600 billion spent nationwide on education at all levels each year, an increasing percentage goes toward the purchase of computers, calculators, Internet access, audiovisual hardware, educational software, and related technologies. After two decades of computers in classrooms, most schools have computer labs; over 90 percent of schools are connected to the Internet (although the degree of connectivity is open for debate); and over one-third of teachers have Internet access in their classrooms, which their students, by all accounts, use frequently.

At the same time, the use of computers has become widespread in the workplace. In October 1997, 50 percent of all workers used computers on the job, and 89 percent of employees with college degrees find computers an indispensable tool on the job site.

So are we getting our money's worth out of instructional technology? Has learning increased? Are students receiving higher scores on standardized national tests? Forget the scores—are they learning anything at all using computers, the Internet, or fancy technology? Are teachers advancing their own professional development, or are the latest technology-based tools sitting idle most of the school day? Let's take a closer look at the big picture, which involves preparing our teachers, students, and our schools to use technology effectively.

The Technology Facade provides administrators, teachers, technology coordinators, parents, committee members—anyone interested in technology—with an "instruction manual" for a better technology program. The Facade Checklist measures the health of a school's program in three critical areas: its use of technology, the infrastructure in place to suppport technology, and its strategy for technology in teaching and learning. The checklist, and how it is to be administered, is contained within the first two chapters of the book. By the end of Chapter 2, you will have a letter grade to attribute to your program. However, the true value of the book is the remaining chapters, devoted to helping a school secure a better score in each of the three areas. Use the book as a reference. Use the book as a guide. But, most importantly, use the book to become better stewards of your technology resources.

PREPARING OUR TEACHERS

We know from the research that most teachers and students use word processing programs. Yet the percentage of teachers who routinely use spreadsheets, simulations, CAD systems, and multimedia software is in the single digits when national statistics are presented regarding their integration in our children's mathematics, science, and social studies classes.

Education Week surveyed teachers and found that about half of all teachers do not use computers at all in their teaching and do not foresee using computers. About 6 out of 10 teachers have had either no training in using computers or less than 5 hours of training (Orlofsky and Jerald, 1999). And a U.S. Department of Education workshop found that education technology training for teachers is almost always a one-shot seminar—usually an afternoon with an expert or 200 teachers in the gym (National Center for Education Statistics [NCES], 1999).

The latter sentiment from teachers is echoed by their administrators. Most administrators say they do not have enough money to train teachers on computer use and cannot afford to give them time off for training. It takes teacher training—a good deal of it—to put all this new technology to its best use in the classroom. "You can have all the technology in the world, but if you do not invest in teachers and help them acquire the comfort and know-how, it will be wasted," said Linda Roberts (1993), head of the federal Office of Educational Technology. We need to find ways to help teachers be competent, confident, and creative users of technology.

Some states are moving to improve funding for teacher training as they begin to recognize that computers without trained teachers will not be worth much. The lack of teacher training is a major obstacle to the push for computer-assisted learning. The lack of student preparation is another obstacle.

PREPARING OUR STUDENTS

All over America, communities are rushing to infuse technology into the schools so that all students will have access to the benefits of technologically sophisticated classrooms. To properly prepare our students to use computers and technology, we must provide real-world instruction and computer-based activities, manage all activities related to instruction, and streamline operations pertaining to the day-to-day use of technology in the classroom.

Technology is the latest "reform" to come into our schools, riding the crest of a wave that encourages the behavioral, cognitive, and humanistic approaches to teaching and learning. Bloom's taxonomy of educational objectives (Bloom, 1956) still holds many truths for teaching and learning in the twenty-first century. More than ever before, teachers are encouraging knowledge and comprehension using computer-assisted instruction and educational software that encourage students to label, list, classify, and describe. At the higher levels of thinking, office productivity tools and utilities provide an avenue for application and analysis as students use technology to interpret, operate, and analyze. At the highest levels of thinking, synthesis, and evaluation, students find technology to be a useful tool as they assemble, compose, construct, appraise, and argue by using electronic mail to collaborate with peers, Internet-based research to explore in more detail the topics presented by the teacher, and video and audio conferencing to share ideas.

Teaching students word processing, database management, and spreadsheets—or even web page design and multimedia presentations—is seen by many school technologists as part of a new literacy, something students must learn and schools must teach. Schools recognize this growing set of student skills and are taking advantage of the movement to secure the technology they need to provide these skills. But only a few recognize why teaching students effective Internet search strategies may be a more critical and a more basic skill than teaching them to design a web page. It is the application of technology skills for thinking and problem solving that will benefit the school and the workplace.

The Technology Facade makes a significant distinction in its focus on the use of technology as a tool rather than as a specific set of skills and competencies. For the student as well as the teacher, this is an extremely critical distinction that the reader must appreciate before applying the Technology Facade Checklist and continuing further in this book.

PREPARING OUR SCHOOLS

U.S. school districts planned to spend about $5.2 billion on educational technology in the 2000–2001 school year, 21 percent more than in 1999–2000. A report released by the research firm Quality Education Data also revealed that nearly half of school districts surveyed planned to spend more on software—up from 34 percent. Increases in spending were mainly for CD-ROMs to run on the modern multimedia computers used now in most schools (almost half of which were purchased in 1999 and 2000). Hardware expenditures were projected to increase in 41 percent of school districts, and most hardware expenditures are for personal computers and network servers (1999).

Only recently has research offered us a recommended model for considering costs associated with an instructional technology program. The model involves the following:

- *Connection to school.* External connection costs include installation and access and usage charges for both the school and the district.
- *Connection within school.* Internal connection costs include the materials and labor for installing local area networks (e.g., cabling and network interface cards), as well as file servers, hubs, and routers.
- *Hardware.* These costs include multimedia-capable computers, printers, scanners, furniture stations, and security systems. They also include any facility upgrades or retrofitting required in older schools,

including electricity and air-conditioning systems. In addition to each computer, two printers and a scanner for each computer lab, and one printer and one scanner per classroom are considered. Furniture and security equipment must also be considered.

- *Content.* Content costs include prepackaged software and access and usage charges for online services. Software upgrades depend on the particular package or service.
- *Professional development.* These costs include substitute teachers to cover times when teachers are out for training, as well as support resources for the computer lab and the classroom shared to help teachers integrate the technology into the curriculum. Costs for the training courses themselves were also included.
- *Systems operation.* Systems operation costs include resources dedicated to designing and operating the technology.

National surveys (*Connecting K–12 Schools to the Information Superhighway,* 1999) conducted using this model found a staggering price tag for the implementation and integration of technology in our schools.

MODEL	NATIONAL COSTS (BILLIONS OF DOLLARS)		COST PER SCHOOL (THOUSANDS OF DOLLARS)		COST PER STUDENT (DOLLARS)	
	Initial	*Ongoing*	*Initial*	*Ongoing*	*Initial*	*Ongoing*
Computer Labs	11	4	125	45	225	80
Computers in the Classroom	47	14	555	165	975	255
Libraries	29	8	340	90	610	155
Total	**87**	**26**	**1,020**	**300**	**1,810**	**490**

Even so, the costs of installing and supporting that technology represent a small portion of the public education budget. Each school and district must make considered choices about how much to invest in technology, how best to achieve its educational goals, and how fast it wishes to deploy (and remain current with) the technology. Across all schools, the pace of deployment and the realization of educational benefits will remain strongly influenced by three factors: the availability of funding, professional development opportunities for teachers and staff, and the pace of courseware development.

READY TO TACKLE THE TECHNOLOGY FACADE?

The good news is that the Technology Facade can be conquered—once its effects, components, and vulnerabilities are realized. And that's what this book is all about. At its best, technology facilitates deep exploration and integration of information, high-level thinking, and profound engagement by allowing students to design, explore, experiment, access information, and model complex phenomena. And that's what we all want for our schools, our teachers, and our students—the best!

NOTE

To contribute to the research, checklist results can be forwarded to the author either anonymously or with attribution, for inclusion in revisions to this text. Copies of the checklist may be forwarded either electronically to tomei@duq.edu or via mail to the following address:

> Lawrence A. Tomei
> Director, Program in Instructional Technology
> 327A Fisher Hall
> Duquesne University
> Pittsburgh, PA 15282

ACKNOWLEDGMENTS

The author wishes to acknowledge members of the Duquesne University School of Education ILEAD 1997 cohort who began the discussion of technology scenarios in schools and created several of the situations used in this book to describe the Technology Facade. Also, thanks to the many teachers, corporate trainers, and educators in the Duquesne University Program in Instructional Technology who contributed to the 20 items which now comprise the checklist. It is not often that teachers and students get the opportunity to collaborate on the creation of a new tool that may impact the future of classroom instruction. The Technology Facade is just such an idea and each of these individuals is to be commended for their role.

Many thanks to the following reviewers: Maria Teresa Fernandez, United States International University; and Jim Huff, California State University, Chico.

BIBLIOGRAPHY

Bloom, Benjamin. *Taxonomy of Educational Objectives*. Upper Saddle River, NJ: Addison-Wesley, 1956.

McKinsey and Company, Inc. *Connecting K–12 Schools to the Information Superhighway*. California: Author, 1999.

National Center For Education Statistics, U.S. Department of Education, Office of Educational Research and Improvement. *Examining Teacher Quality: Good Preparation and Continuing Development Help Teachers Meet Education Challenges*. Washington, DC: Author, 1998a.

———. *Internet Access in Public Schools and Classrooms: 1994–98*. Washington, DC: Author, February 1999.

———. "Learning Resources and Technology," *Digest of Education Statistics*. 1998b. Retrieved November 13, 2000 from http://nces.ed.gov/pubs99/digest98/d98t428.html

———. "Training, A Necessary Investment in Staff," *Safeguarding Your Technology*. 1998c. Retrieved November 13, 2000 from http://nces.ed.gov/pubs98/safetech/chapter10.html

Orlofsky, Greg F., and Jerald, Craig D. "Raising the Bar on School Technology," *Education Week*, September 23, 1999.

Quality Education Data, Inc. "Ten Trends to Watch in Instructional Technology." 2000. Retrieved November 13, 2000 from www.qeddata.com

Roberts, Linda G. "Toward the Classroom of the 21st Century," from Reinventing Schools National Conference, May 10, 1993. Audio file retrieved from www.nap.edu/readingroom/books/techgap

U.S. Census Bureau. *Home Ownership of Computers, By Population Classification*. Washington, DC: U.S. Government Printing Office, 1997.

Websites about Bloom's Taxonomy

www.dlrn.org/library/dl/guide4.html

Skills levels of Bloom's Taxonomy
www.coun.uvic.ca/learn/program/hndouts/bloom.html

Bloom et al.'s Taxonomy of the Cognitive Domain
www.valdosta.peachnet.edu/~whuitt/psy702/cogsys/bloom.html

www.che.wsu.edu/~millerrc/bloom.html

www.ceap.wcu.edu/Houghton/Learner/think/bloomsTaxonomy.html

■ ■ ■ ■ ■

PART I

INTRODUCING THE TECHNOLOGY FACADE

Are taxpayers getting their money's worth from all the technology being infused into our schools? Can anyone show that student learning has increased as a result of computer labs and multimedia classrooms? Are teachers even using the latest technology-based tools, or are all but a few avoiding technology? Is this all a hoax being perpetrated on an educational system already overburdened by rising student population and a diminishing tax base? Is this billion-dollar investment we are making simply another passing fad doomed to follow the path of such infamous educational initiatives as the "new math," the open classroom, and outcome-based education?

If the Technology Facade is present in our schools, there is something that can be done about it now. As parents, educators, taxpayers, community leaders, technologists, and concerned citizens, we can change the course of technology in our schools for the betterment of administrators, teachers, and, most importantly, students.

Are any of the following scenarios found in your school?

☑ SCENARIO CHECKLIST

Our computer lab sports systems with the latest processors, the fastest CD-ROM players, the largest memory capacities, and the most sophisticated multimedia sound systems. But only a few teachers use the lab, and then only when the computer teacher "lets them."

☐ You will find this scenario in my school.

☐ This scenario does not describe my school.

Our state-of-the-art computer lab is filled with Macintosh or Windows personal computers. But students are not permitted in the lab during study halls or after school, teachers must locate the secreted key ring that unlocks the three padlocks on the door, and no one is allowed to use the machines unless the computer teacher is present.

☐ You will find this scenario in my school.
☐ This scenario does not describe my school.

Our school handbook contains a technology section lauding the expensive inventory of hardware and software recently purchased and installed courtesy of the local PTA. But after nearly two years of bake sales, candy drives, and magazine campaigns, the only way to obtain new software or hardware upgrades is from year-end funds the school does not spend on its "regular" programs.

☐ You will find this scenario in my school.
☐ This scenario does not describe my school.

Our school has the most up-to-date technology available. No other school in our district compares with our computers, network, or educational software library. Yet not a single teacher, much less any member of the staff, has attended anything but an initial in-service training session (and that was over 6 months ago) to learn how to operate the technology. Students understand more about these tools than their teachers do, and the teachers know it.

☐ You will find this scenario in my school.
☐ This scenario does not describe my school.

The technology coordinator briefs visiting dignitaries on the benefits of computers to our school. No one asks the teachers their opinions. As a matter of fact, the nominal Technology Committee does not even include a classroom teacher (other than the computer teacher) much less a parent, community leader, alumnus, or (horrors!) a student.

☐ You will find this scenario in my school.
☐ This scenario does not describe my school.

The principal tours our school with the parents of next year's prospective batch of incoming students, promoting Mrs. Schnieder's daily computer classes for all students. But a closer look finds outdated hardware, obsolete software, and a graveyard of broken parts and pieces in a locked cabinet. Nearly every student boasts a better computer setup at home.

☐ You will find this scenario in my school.
☐ This scenario does not describe my school.

Where is the school's technology plan? In a routine visit with the principal to discuss upcoming technology projects that include upgrades to the computer lab and connection of all classroom computers to the Internet, dust flies from the binder holding the plan, and its cover page reads, "Last Revised in 19xx"—over four years ago—when the last lab upgrade was completed.

☐ You will find this scenario in my school.

☐ This scenario does not describe my school.

Teachers complain about lack of access to the school's computer lab for special in-class projects. Looking more closely, we find that school policy calls for every class to spend 2 hours in computers every week. Let's see . . . the lab is open 6 hours a day; that's three classes per day on average, and we have 15 classes in the building. That leaves—absolutely no time for anything else! But without a list of skills and competencies for each grade level, how do we know that a first grader needs as much exposure to computers as our eighth graders? Chances are, they don't!

☐ You will find this scenario in my school.

☐ This scenario does not describe my school.

Do any or all of these scenarios sound familiar? If so, welcome to the Technology Facade. But make no mistake, this book will not take the reader on a guided tour through the back lot of a famous movie studio, with its false fronts and hollowed out sets. It will not dwell on the shortfalls of shiny computer labs, unprepared teachers, overworked technology coordinators, and last-minute budget readjustments. This book is not about abandoning technology.

Rather, its purpose is to celebrate the innovators who have brought powerful technological tools into our schools and classrooms. It honors the pioneer who seeks to demonstrate the positive impact of technology on student learning. And, it seeks to gauge the health of a school's technology program so that the principles of sound fiscal management and human resources offered in this book are applied toward the successful outcome of a well-designed technology program.

CHAPTER 1

DEFINING THE TECHNOLOGY FACADE

> *The Technology Facade: "The use of technology in a school or school district without benefit of the necessary infrastructure to adequately support its use as a viable instructional strategy."*

By definition, the Technology Facade encompasses three critical elements. First, the Technology Facade occurs when we fail to understand that technology itself is not the goal; even educational technology falls short of the pedagogical impact of computers in the classroom. To avoid the pitfalls of the Technology Facade, schools must embrace the more inclusive *use of instructional technology* as a way of focusing attention on all aspects of the teaching and learning process.

Second, the Technology Facade occurs when we fail to understand that technology is an ongoing process that demands the time, attention, and dedication of an entire *infrastructure* consisting of many competent people; a significant and consistent level of financial investment; and a commitment of resources that will necessarily be diverted from other critical schoolwide obligations.

Third, the Technology Facade occurs when we fail to understand that instructional technology is another *instructional strategy*—another tool for teaching elementary, secondary, or adult learners.

To avoid the Technology Facade, teachers, staff, administrators, parents, and students must come to appreciate the advantages and limitations that technology provides to the learning environment. Educators must come to grips with a working definition of the Facade and its components; a rubric for evaluating its effects; and a process for conducting, analyzing, and assessing its impact on a school or district.

> ## The Technology Facade: "The use of technology in a school or school district without benefit of the necessary infrastructure to adequately support its use as a viable instructional strategy."

"THE USE OF TECHNOLOGY IN A SCHOOL OR SCHOOL DISTRICT"

U.S. school districts spent about $5.2 billion on technology in the 1999–2000 school year—21 percent more than in the previous year. The research firm Quality Education Data (2000) reports the largest planned increase of this magnitude since technology was formally recognized in our schools over four decades ago. The organization's report revealed that

- Hardware expenditures are projected to increase in 41 percent of the districts. However, significant outlays are being made in related classroom technology such as calculators, projection systems, white boards, laser and video players, classroom ergonomics, and distance-learning hardware.
- After an 18-month period in which almost half of the school districts surveyed purchased new educational technology, most expenditures are for personal computers and Internet servers.
- Nearly half of school districts plan to spend more on software—up from a previous 34 percent. Increases in software spending are mainly for CD-ROM–based instructional technology to run on modern multimedia computers now in most schools.

Three terms are often used interchangeably, and mistakenly, when discussing technology in the classroom. A common misconception held by many educators and technologists alike is that the terms *technology, educational technology,* and *instructional technology* are synonymous—they are not.

Technology

"Technology is the application of behavioral and physical sciences concepts and other knowledge to the solution of problems" (Gentry, 1995, 2). It can be said that technology is value free; that is, the mere presence of technology is neither good nor bad, effective nor ineffective, an inevitable success nor a failure. When applied to learning, technology encompasses all aspects of education that impact the student. Bus transportation and heat and cooling systems, for example, contribute directly to successful learning outcomes and, therefore, may influence the Technology Facade as much as computers in the classroom, the videocassette player, or cable television.

Educational Technology

Educational technology is "the combination of instructional, developmental, managerial, and other technologies as applied specifically to the solution of educational problems" (Gentry, 1995, 4). Educational technology goes beyond the idea of general problem solving to the more specific advancement of student learning. Examples include accounting software that tracks tuition payments, a language arts reading lab, or even a gymnasium weight room. Each influences teaching and learning and, therefore, the Technology Facade.

Instructional Technology

Instructional Technology, or "the application of educational technologies to the solution of specific instructional problems" (Gentry, 1995, 5), combines educational technology with learning strategies, developmental principles, and pedagogical ideals.

> *The Technology Facade: "The use of technology in a school or school district without benefit of **the necessary infrastructure to adequately support its use** as a viable instructional strategy."*

"THE NECESSARY INFRASTRUCTURE TO ADEQUATELY SUPPORT ITS USE"

Every teacher can recite the "three R's" of education. And, every first year business student can recount the basic management premise, which stresses the importance of the "three M's"—men, money, and material, or, to be more politically correct, people, finances, and resources. In some combination, aspects of these elements are part of every successful business venture. For the

Technology Facade, too, they make a contribution when we consider the many applications of technology for teaching and learning.

People of the Technology Facade

The most complex element of the Technology Facade is people. Teachers implement instructional technology in the classroom, and student learning outcomes remain the focus of these efforts. But teachers and students are not the only players; Table 1.1 lists other people involved in the Technology Facade.

There are undoubtedly others who do not appear in Table 1.1 and, of course, this list is not intended to reflect order of importance. Each individual has a critical role in determining whether technology is welcomed in the school and, later, whether that welcome is nurtured into a viable, continuing relationship that benefits student learning.

Surprisingly, faculty and students are often overlooked as prospective members of a school's technology team. While students interact with computers in the classroom, teachers are expected to embrace technology, often fending for themselves when it comes to training. A sound technology program—one that tears down the false fronts of the Technology Facade—addresses the concerns, needs, contributions, and training requirements of all who will be using the technology.

Finances of the Technology Facade

The necessary infrastructure for classroom technology depends, of course, on a budget. Fiscal and monetary shortcomings are often the first signals of the Technology Facade. Budgets should include a specific technology line item in the annual request for funds. A sure sign of the Facade is the use of "fallout" monies to fund lab upgrades and software purchases. Funding for technology support staff, faculty incentive programs, and periodic in-service training

TABLE 1.1   People of the Technology Facade

EDUCATORS/ ADMINISTRATORS	STAFF	CLIENTS	COMMUNITY AND OTHER INTERESTED PARTIES
District superintendent	Teachers	Parents	Community leaders
Technology coordinators	Budget manager	Students	Curriculum designers
School principal	School librarians		
School board members			

programs are evidence that the Facade is being torn down and replaced with a solid technology program.

Resources of the Technology Facade

Consider for a moment all the elements necessary for a competent technology program. Computer labs involve dozens of machines and hundreds of software applications, with new and emerging technologies being touted incessantly by eager vendors. Internet connections require a fiber optic cable backbone and network servers, plus a knowledgeable coordinator who can ensure uninterrupted service. Professional development in technology-related training endeavors demands a significant commitment of time and effort by teachers, administrators, and staff. Library, community, parents, and corporate sponsors are integral to any successful technology program. Data must be collected and analyzed, reports must be prepared and presented, and assessments must be administered and validated before the more technical decisions can be made. And then there's the technology plan—a voluminous document describing the past, present, and future of technology in a school plant. The plan must be prepared, approved, implemented, reevaluated, and revised if the school's technology future is to mature.

Educators know all too well that there are only so many resources to go around. Technology is not the only program that deserves a fair share of resources. In the business world, it is the artful manager who knows how to balance the three M's to produce the desired outcomes. To avoid the pitfalls of the Technology Facade, schools must commit to building the necessary infrastructure to ensure that instructional technology remains a viable focus in support of the teaching and learning process.

> *The Technology Facade: "The use of technology in a school or school district without benefit of the necessary infrastructure to adequately support its use as **a viable instructional strategy.**"*

"A VIABLE INSTRUCTIONAL STRATEGY"

Teachers design, develop, and deliver instruction; and technology-based instruction is no different. As with other instructional strategies, it encompasses the dimensions of curriculum, classroom instruction, and student assessment. Any documented successes with instructional technology have gone on to demonstrate that technology is simply another tool for learning. A clear understanding of curricular direction, lesson goals, learning objectives, and student learning styles must precede any development of technology-based resources. How teachers use technology in the preparation of lesson materials is an excellent indicator of the health of a school's technology program.

However, unlike the volumes of basic pedagogical investigation, research into instructional technology tends to focus on hardware and software, contributing little to the larger and more challenging dimension of learning how technology addresses key elements of teaching and learning. Perhaps this book will contribute to the research in the critical areas of practice and pedagogy.

SUMMARY

The Technology Facade is defined as the use of technology without the necessary infrastructure to support its application as an instructional strategy. At its foundation, instructional technology is sustained by administrators, school board members, community leaders, teachers, and students who support and embrace these newest instructional tools. It must be nurtured by a dependable source of funds and resources, and it must become an integral component of school curriculum.

Masquerade or reality, it all comes down to choices. Shiny computer labs, or a viable technology program; computers in every classroom, or an in-service program that supports teacher-developed instruction; a public relations program, or a sound academic curriculum; walking tours of computer classrooms, or teachers that demonstrate the importance of teaching with technology. The purpose of this book is to help schools identify the strengths and weaknesses of their technology programs and to pinpoint ways to make them better.

BIBLIOGRAPHY

Gentry, Cass G. "Educational Technology: A Question of Meaning." In G. Anglin (Ed.), *Instructional Technology: Past, Present, and Future,* 2nd ed. Englewood, CO: Libraries Unlimited, 1995.
Quality Education Data, Inc. "Ten Trends to Watch in Instructional Technology." 2000. Retrieved November 13, 2000 from www.qeddata.com

CHAPTER 2

THE TECHNOLOGY
FACADE CHECKLIST

The Technology Facade Checklist (see Appendix 2.1 at the end of this chapter) examines the health of a school's instructional technology program. Once applied and scored, it is augmented by the remaining parts of this book, which suggest a step-by-step strategy for resolving any identified shortcomings. Each step and recommendation provided in Chapters 4 through 12 is backed by research, practical treatment, and a history of personal application.

For best results, the Technology Facade Checklist should be applied by several members of a school's technology committee, preferably independently of one another and at varied times throughout the academic school year. Apply the checklist as close to the beginning of the academic year as possible to allow the composite score to become a benchmark. The last full month of school, usually May, should be targeted for a second application of the checklist. A follow-up survey allows members of the administration and the technology committee to compare the results of their year-long effort against their original expectations and set a course for change during the summer months before the beginning and the start of the next academic year.

After conducting the checklist, consider whether to release the final numerical score to school administrators, school board members, or even other members of the technology committee. Particularly when using the checklist for the first time, the resulting composite score may be discouraging and actually produce a negative attitude about the chances of overcoming the Facade. Key players on the strategic technology planning team may need to know the A through F rating if the revised technology plan is to address identified shortcomings.

CONDUCTING THE SURVEY

This chapter proposes an eight-step process for applying the Technology Facade Checklist. Each step should be followed in order and documented in the minutes of the Technology Committee meetings to ensure compliance and avoid misunderstandings among the key players.

Step 1: Contact the School Administrator and Secure Permission to Conduct the Survey

Do not attempt to accomplish the Checklist without first obtaining the permission of the school principal or district superintendent if this is to be a districtwide examination. The Checklist is not a tool for one-upmanship; the effects of the Technology Facade can be reduced only if there is an atmosphere of trust and cooperation among all interested parties. It is best if permission is obtained in writing. Offer the administrator right of first rebuttal once the survey is completed and before the points are awarded.

Appendix 2.2 at the end of this chapter presents an example letter to the school principal requesting approval to conduct the survey. A letter requesting approval should contain the following, as a minimum: the dates during which the survey will be applied, request for a separate meeting with teachers to discuss the status of the technology program, a point of contact for the survey (usually the computer teacher or technology coordinator), procedures for returning the endorsed approval, and a draft of an endorsement statement ready for the principal's signature.

Step 2: Make an Appointment with the Technology Coordinator

The technology coordinator or computer teacher probably has the most information about the program along with the most corporate memory regarding the various technologies found in the school. Several of the questions in the Checklist depend on collaboration with the senior technology director in the school. For example, Is the computer teacher the only educator who dispenses technology-related instruction (Question 1)? Are the computer facilities in your school locked or available during periods such as recess, study halls, lunch, and before and after school (Question 2)? Are the school computers located in the library, classrooms, or computer lab (Question 3)? How is technology funded in your school (Question 11)? Is there a technology plan for the school (Question 13)?

Step 3: Apply the Survey and Complete the Checklist

Completing the Checklist requires approximately 2 to 3 hours and may be divided into several periods. However, the entire checklist should be completed within a couple of days to avoid classroom, teacher, and student interruptions that could detract from the validity of the responses. Here are several considerations when conducting the survey:

- If a member of the technology committee volunteers to personally conduct the Technology Facade checklist, respectfully decline in favor of a more independent surveyor. It is unlikely that teachers, students and staff will provide unbiased comments; besides, even the hint of impropriety should be avoided (Henry, 1997).
- If any part of the Checklist is to be completed and returned by mail, enclose a self-addressed envelope. Otherwise, the recipient will almost certainly throw the checklist straight into the trash can.
- If results can be collected anonymously, do so. In this case, make it clear to potential respondents that anonymity is assured. Even if names are not requested, participants are reassured by a statement of confidentiality.
- In many cases, participants are asked to reply on behalf of the school. Understand that doing so may inhibit potential responders from providing their true feelings regarding technology.
- People will not complete the questionnaire if they think it is a waste of their time. People are more likely to think this if the questionnaire is poorly presented. The surveyor must be an individual who has the trust and confidence of respondents, especially regarding technology. Ensure the surveyor understands and can explain all the terms used in the Checklist.
- Reserve those questions pertaining to the school's funding of technology to the business manager or principal. A teacher or administrator who is not prepared to answers these questions is unlikely to provide accurate information. On the other hand, people who are really in a position to answer such questions may prefer not to; give them some assurance that this information will not compromise the school's position with respect to technology funding.
- Avoid bias. A survey is biased if its outcome has been influenced by factors other than the one being studied. Bias is occasionally overt; more than likely, the surveyor is simply not open-minded about the results received, and chooses to interpret them incorrectly.

Step 4: Validate the Points Awarded

Each question and each section of the Technology Facade Checklist contributes points to the overall composite score. Section I of the Checklist, "The Use of Technology," assesses the extent of technology in the school and awards 55 points, or 27.5 percent of the total available 200 points. Section II,

"The Necessary Infrastructure," evaluates the people, funds, and resources of the technology program and awards 104 points, or 52 percent of the total available points. Section III, "A Viable Instructional Strategy," deals with the integration of technology as a teaching and learning strategy and awards the final 41 points, or 20.5 percent of the points available.

Several questions are exclusive in nature; that is, there is only one set of points awarded. For this type of question, the Checklist instructs the surveyor to "Select one" of the responses and transfer the points to the box identified as "Your Score." Question 2 is an example (see Figure 2.1). The arrow (➡) directs the surveyor to the proper location on the Checklist for filling in the points awarded. Note that the "Points Awarded" column is shaded to indicate that only one response should be selected.

Other questions are inclusive, and a program may receive up to a maximum number of points. For these questions, identified by "Select all that apply," examine each of the items to ensure that the correct number of points are awarded. Question 3 is an example of this type of question (see Figure 2.2). No shading appears in the "Points Awarded" column because all responses can be selected. The arrow (➡) again directs the surveyor to the "Your Score" location for recording the total points.

Step 5: Complete the Comprehensive Analysis Form

A valuable contribution to the Technology Facade process is the Comprehensive Analysis Form containing each of the three elements comprising the

FIGURE 2.1   **Example of *Select One* Question**

2. **Are the computer facilities in your school . . . ? Select one.** *(You can find out more about this question in Chapter 3.)*

	Points Available	Points Awarded
Locked during unsupervised periods such as recess, study halls, lunch, and before and after school	0	
Available before and/or after school	3	
Available when there are no classes scheduled	5	
Open during recess, study halls, lunch, and before and after school	7	
Your Score (7 possible)	➡	

FIGURE 2.2   Example of *Select All That Apply* Question

---

3. **School computers are located in our . . . : Select all that apply.** *(You can find out more about this question in Chapter 3.)*

	Points Available	Points Awarded
Library	1	
Classrooms	3	
Computer lab	3	
Your Score (7 possible)	➡	

Checklist. This form is divided into three Facade elements: Section I, Use of Technology in a School or School District (items 1 through 6); Section II, the Necessary Infrastructure to Support Its Use (items 7 through 15); and Section III, Viable Instructional Strategy (items 16 through 20).

After completing each of the twenty questions in the Checklist, tally the points awarded in each of the elements and transfer the totals to Column D of the Analysis Form. In the example form shown in Figure 2.3, the scores of 40, 82, and 12 were transferred from the Checklist.

Next, total Column D to determine the number of points a school received out of the 200 possible points. Again, Figure 2.3 shows a composite total score of 134 points.

Next, use the Comprehensive Analysis Form to determine how the three elements stack up in the particular school or district. Which of the three is the strongest (i.e., greatest percentage of Checklist points), and which is the weakest? In the example, 40 out of 55 points are converted into 72.7 percent for the school's Use of Technology score. The Necessary Infrastructure score accounts for 82 out of a possible 104 points, or 78.8 percent of the possible points. And the Viable Instructional Strategy score is represented by 29.3 percent (12 out of a possible 41 points). Complete Column E with these percentages.

Complete Column F by circling the proper ranking of each element according to the highest percentage score depicted in Column E. In the example, the school surveyed performed best in The Necessary Infrastructure at 78.8 percent, followed by its Use of Technology at 72.7 percent, and a dismal performance in the Viable Instructional Strategy area. The Analysis Form makes it very easy to pinpoint the major causes of the Technology Facade within a particular school.

FIGURE 2.3   **Example Checklist Analysis Form**

Comprehensive Checklist Analysis Form

(Complete the shaded areas in the table to determine your composite score in the Technology Facade.)

		Points Accumulated		Percentages Awarded	
Facade Element	*Checklist Items*	*Possible Points*	*Fill in Points Awarded*	*Fill in Percentage*	*Circle Ranking*
Use of Technology in a School or School District	Items 1 through 6	55 points	40	72.7	1 ② 3
The Necessary Infrastructure	Items 7 through 15	104 points	82	78.8	① 2 3
A Viable Instructional Strategy	Items 16 through 20	41 points	12	29.3	1 2 ③
Totals		200	134	100%	

Step 6: Calculate the Composite Score and Determine the Facade Rating

Transfer the total number of points identified in Column D and complete the Composite Score Form. Figure 2.4 shows how a composite score of 134 points was moved to the new form, and a Facade Rating of B– was awarded.

FIGURE 2.4   **Example Composite Score Form**

Composite Score Form

Total Possible Points: 200   *Your Composite Score:* _134_   *Your Facade Rating:* _B–_

175–200 points	Outstanding Technology Program	A Rating
125–175	Satisfactory Technology Program	B Rating
100–125	Modest Phase of the Technology Facade	C Rating
75–100	Moderate Phase of the Technology Facade	D Rating
< 75	Severe Phase of the Technology Facade	F Rating

Step 7: Provide the Results to the Decision Makers

Do not be too disappointed with the Facade rating first time out; very few schools merit higher than a C+ rating in their initial survey. Actually, initial research using the checklist (n = 242 schools) found only 5.2 percent of the respondents merited an A rating, 11.6 percent secured a B rating, nearly 65 percent received a C rating, and the remaining 19 percent received the two lowest ratings.

After all the scores are transferred to the forms, the results of the survey may be shared with administrators, teachers, staff, and the technology committee as soon as possible. Delays only fuel speculations that contribute to misunderstandings and anxieties. Include the minimum amount of data that communicates the overall findings effectively. Only the senior administrators (e.g., the principal and perhaps the technology coordinator or computer teacher) need to see the actual completed Checklist. It is not usually helpful to report every response to everyone on the staff; a summary is sufficient.

Although the Checklist has the appearance of an objective evaluation instrument, it is important to recognize that many of the questions, not to mention the points, are subjective in nature. Reading the results of any survey requires the individual to distinguish between numerical points and any personal interpretations.

The Comprehensive Analysis Form and the Composite Score Form do two things: First, they present consistent, easy-to-understand, nontechnical results to interested readers. Second, they convert the results of the survey into the rudimentary elements of an action plan for change.

Step 8: Begin a Continuous Improvement Program

A worthwhile improvement plan is based on continuous, steady progress toward the ultimate goal. The Technology Facade Checklist measures that progress and, once accomplished, becomes the impetus for a sound program of continuous improvement mirroring Deming's total quality management (TQM) philosophy.

Deming discusses the possible transformation of educators (Joiner and Scholtes, 1999), stating that they must become leaders instead of bosses, coaches instead of enforcers. They must focus on solving problems and constantly improving instead of blaming and controlling. The quality-focused approach to educational leadership requires continuous feedback from the customer (i.e., the student and parent), and constant communications and feedback within and among units of the organization—that is, the various grade levels and academic content areas.

CONCLUSION

The Technology Facade Checklist is the product of much research and study. Its major qualification stems from previous, repeated applications in dozens of schools and school districts. Even so, the Checklist remains a living document to be improved by even more applications and ever closer scrutiny by the technology community.

Please modify the questions and the suggested points (especially the points!) to serve the specific needs of your institution. Remember, however, that the intent of the Checklist is not to make the school "feel good" about technology—that would only serve to enhance the Facade. Rather, its purpose is to improve programs by addressing areas that would produce the best results.

BIBLIOGRAPHY

Gentry, Cass G. "The Field: History and Overview." In G. Anglin (Ed.), *Instructional Technology: Past, Present, and Future*, 2nd ed. Englewood, CO: Libraries Unlimited, 1995.

Henry, Tamara. "Big Jump in Budgets to Get Technology in the Classroom," *USA Today*, July 21, 1997.

Joiner, Brian L., and Scholtes, Peter R. *Total Quality Leadership vs. Management by Results*. 1999. Retrieved November 13, 2000 from the Deming Electronic Network Web Site BBS: http://deming.eng.clemson.edu/pub/den/files/tql.zip

Appendix 2.1

Technology Facade Checklist

Instructions: Complete each of the following questions by entering the most appropriate response and transferring the points to "Your Score."

I. THE USE OF TECHNOLOGY

School districts plan to spend more on technology in the upcoming years, the largest planned increase since technology was formally recognized in our schools over four decades ago. Are the key players in your school coming on board? Answer items 1–6 to assess the extent of technology use in your school. Total available points for this section of the Checklist is 55.

1. **Are the technologies in your school used by classroom teachers, or is the computer teacher the only educator who dispenses technology-**

related instruction? Select one. *(You can find out more about this question in Chapter 3.)*

	Points Available	Points Awarded
Computer teacher only	1	
A few teachers use technology, but not regularly	3	
A few teachers use technology routinely	5	
Technology is routinely used by many classroom teachers	7	
Your Score (7 possible)	➡	

2. **Are the computer facilities in your school . . . ? Select one.** *(You can find out more about this question in Chapter 3.)*

	Points Available	Points Awarded
Locked during unsupervised periods such as recess, study halls, lunch, and before and after school	0	
Available before and/or after school	3	
Available when there are no classes scheduled	5	
Open during recess, study halls, lunch, and before and after school	7	
Your Score (7 possible)	➡	

3. **School computers are located in our . . . : Select all that apply.** *(You can find out more about this question in Chapter 3.)*

	Points Available	Points Awarded
Library	1	
Classrooms	3	
Computer lab	3	
Your Score (7 possible)	➡	

4. **Do classroom teachers use technology for . . . ? Rate each separately.**
(You can find out more about this question in Chapter 4.)

	Points Available				Points Awarded
	Never	Seldom	Occasionally	Routinely	
Grading	0	1	3	5	
Lesson preparation	0	1	3	5	
Out-of-class assignments	0	1	3	5	
Professional development	0	1	3	5	
Your Score (20 possible)	➡	➡	➡	➡	

5. **Is the computer teacher expected to have lesson plans with specific student learning objectives related to technology competencies? Select one.** *(You can find out more about this question in Chapter 4.)*

	Points Available	Points Awarded
Computer instruction is not based on lesson plans	0	
Lesson plans are not used. There are general goals for instruction, but no specific learning objectives	1	
Lesson plans contain generic technological competencies and general learning objectives	3	
Detailed lesson plans are used that reflect specific technological competencies expected of each student	7	
Your Score (7 possible)	➡	

6. **Does the software found on your computers reflect current classroom curriculum? Select one.** *(You can find out more about this question in Chapter 5.)*

	Points Available	Points Awarded
Computer software is available, but its selection was not based on teacher input and seldom reflects actual classroom content	1	
Computer software was recently purchased but is not readily available for teachers and students to use	3	
Computer software selection was based on teacher input and its use on current curriculum objectives	5	
Computer software versions are current, software selection is based on teacher input, and the software is routinely used by teachers and students	7	
Your Score (7 possible)	➡	

II. THE NECESSARY INFRASTRUCTURE

Educators know all too well that there are only so many resources to go around. Technology is not the only program deserving of a fair share of resources. To avoid the pitfalls of the Technology Facade, schools must commit to building the necessary infrastructure of people, funds, and resources to ensure that instructional technology remains a viable focus in support of the teaching and learning process. Answer items 7–15 to assess the steadfastness of the technology infrastructure in your school. Total available points for this section of the Checklist is 104.

7. **What is the extent of technology training received by teachers? Select all that apply.** *(You can find out more about this question in Chapter 6.)*

	Points Available	Points Awarded
Initial training over 6 months old	0	
Initial training only within the last 6 months	1	
In-service training on technology at least twice a year	3	

	Points Available	Points Awarded
At least two teachers per school are encouraged to enroll in formal instructional technology programs	3	
Training classes available on demand, scheduled with the technology coordinator	5	
Your Score (12 possible)	➡	

8. **Do teachers participate on the Technology Committee and its subordinate teams? Identify all that apply.** *(You can find out more about this question in Chapter 6.)*

	Points Available	Points Awarded
Teachers do not participate as full voting members	0	
Teachers participate as members of the Hardware/Software Acquisition Team	3	
Teachers participate as members of the Technology Budget Preparation Team	3	
Teachers participate as members of the Instructional Technology Curriculum Team	5	
Teachers participate as members of the Strategic Technology Planning Team	5	
Your Score (16 possible)	➡	

9. **Do parents, community leaders, alumni, and students participate on the Technology Committee and its subordinate teams? Identify all that apply.** *(You can find out more about this question in Chapter 6.)*

	Points Available	Points Awarded
They do not participate as voting members	0	
They participate as members of the Hardware/Software Acquisition Team	3	

They participate as members of the Technology Budget Preparation Team	3	
They participate as members of the Instructional Technology Curriculum Team	5	
They participate as members of the Strategic Technology Planning Team	5	
Your Score (16 possible)	➡	

10. **Does your school provide direct access to the following technology professionals? Identify all that apply.** *(You can find out more about this question in Chapter 6.)*

	Points Available	Points Awarded
None of these professionals are employed in our school	0	
Computer teacher (Part time/Full time)	3/7	
Technology coordinator (Full time only)	5	
Computer technician (Part time/Full time)	1/3	
Network administrator (Full time only)	3	
Your Score (18 possible)	➡	

11. **How is technology funded in your school? Select one.** *(You can find out more about this question in Chapter 7.)*

	Points Available	Points Awarded
Technology is funded with year-end fallout money	1	
Technology is included in the operating budget under a miscellaneous account	3	
Technology is included in the general operating budget	5	

Technology is its own specific, recurring line item in the annual budget	7	
Your Score (7 possible)	➡	

12. **Has your school implemented a recognition program for teachers who develop technology-based instructional materials? Select one.** *(You can find out more about this question in Chapter 7.)*

	Points Available	Points Awarded
There is no remuneration or recognition program to recognize excellence in instructional technology	0	
Excellence in instructional technology is recognized in school newsletters, bulletins, and school board reports	1	
A formal awards program recognizes teachers who develop excellent instructional technology programs	5	
Teachers receive compensatory time, monetary compensation, or other specific remuneration for developing technology-based programs	7	
Your Score (7 possible)	➡	

13. **Is there a technology plan for the school? Select one.** *(You can find out more about this question in Chapter 8.)*

	Points Available	Points Awarded
No technology plan exists in our school	0	
The school is working under a general districtwide plan, but a local building plan does not exist	1	
The school is working on an informal strategy for technology, but a formal plan has not been prepared	3	

Yes, but it is in serious need of revision or has not been revised in the previous 2 years	5	
Yes, and it is revised on a regularly scheduled basis at least annually	7	
Your Score (7 possible)	➡	

14. **Does your school's Technology Plan contain the following? Identify all that apply.** *(You can find out more about this question in Chapter 8.)*

	Points Available	Points Awarded
No technology plan exists in our school	0	
Vision/mission statement	1	
Demographic review of teachers, students, and community	1	
Technology-related purchasing procedures	1	
Periodic and on-call maintenance for instructional technologies used for classroom teaching	1	
Security plan regarding physical threats, human threats, and Internet threats to technology	1	
Formation and operation of a viable technology committee with diverse membership	2	
Impact of technology integration on the curriculum	2	
The uses of technology for lifelong learning, special needs learners, and exceptional learners	2	
A comprehensive facility plan for installation and periodic upgrades	2	
A formal plan for continuous evaluation, both formal and informal	3	
Your Score (16 possible)	➡	

15. **Rate the computers in your school computer lab and classrooms. Identify all that apply.** *(You can find out more about this question in Chapter 8.)*

	Points Available	Points Awarded
Most of the machines are less than 3 years old	1	
Most of the machines are CD-ROM–capable	1	
Most of the machines are connected to printers	1	
Most of the machines are connected to the Internet	2	
Your Score (5 possible)	➡	

III. A VIABLE INSTRUCTIONAL STRATEGY

An understanding of instructional technology and the foundations of a sound support infrastructure are keys to the final step in breaking down the Technology Facade. Answer items 16–20 to assess how seriously your school is taking the integration of technology as a teaching and learning strategy. Total available points for this section of the Checklist is 41.

16. **Has your school developed a scope and sequence specifically addressing student technology competencies? Select one.** *(You can find more about this question in Chapter 9.)*

	Points Available	Points Awarded
No scope and sequence is available	0	
A scope and sequence addressing technology is available only for graduating students (e.g., 8th graders and high school seniors)	3	
A scope and sequence addressing technology is available for selected grades (e.g., 1st, 4th, 8th, 10th, and 12th graders)	5	

A comprehensive scope and sequence addressing technology is available for all students, by grade and subject area	7	
Your Score (7 possible)	➡	

17. **Teachers' lesson plans should include specific learning objectives when using technology-based resources. Is there evidence of learning objectives that are consistent with accepted educational psychology? Select one.** *(You can find more about this question in Chapter 9.)*

	Points Available	Points Awarded
Learning objectives are not identifiable in classroom lesson plans	0	
Learning objectives are used for technology-related lessons, but it is difficult to identify the criteria for successful student learning	1	
Behavioral objectives are used. They include components of behavior (actions to be performed), condition (instructional tools), and criteria (assessment standards)	7	
Cognitive objectives are used. They include components of discovery learning (student-centered growth), constructivism (building of new meaning), and reception learning (structured learning)	7	
Humanistic objectives are used. They include components of individualization (student-tailored instruction), affective education (values training), and intrinsic learning (learning for its own sake)	7	
A combination of behavioral, cognitive, and humanistic learning objectives are used for technology-related lessons. Criteria for successful student learning are readily identified	7	
Your Score (7 possible)	➡	

18. **When using technology-based lessons in the classroom, which of the following resources do teachers personally develop and use for instruction? Identify all that apply.** *(You can find more about this question in Chapter 10.)*

	Points Available	Points Awarded
Text-based materials such as handouts, study guides, and workbooks to guide the lesson	5	
Visual-based presentations, including overhead transparencies to support classroom instruction	5	
Web-based course pages for student exploration and cooperative learning	5	
Your Score (15 possible)	➡	

19. **Describe what typically happens when classroom teachers wish to use technology resources to present a lesson. Select one.** *(You can find more about this question in Chapter 10.)*

	Points Available	Points Awarded
The computer labs or technology resources are often unavailable	0	
The technology teacher or coordinator must present the lesson	1	
Technology must be transported into the classroom for the session	3	
Computer labs or technology resources are available for scheduling without significant delays	5	
Your Score (5 possible)	➡	

20. **How do students* in the computer classroom/laboratory describe their experience? Select one.** *(You can find more about this question in Chapter 11.)*

	Points Available	Points Awarded
Play time or game time	0	
Unstructured, not sure of expected learning outcomes	1	
Applicable to what they are covering in class	5	
Appropriate for current classes and important for required/anticipated future skills	7	
Your Score (7 possible)	➡	

*This question restricted to students and their teachers in grades 6 and above.

Comprehensive Checklist Analysis Form

(Complete the shaded areas in the table to determine your composite score in the Technology Facade.)

		Points Accumulated		Percentages Awarded	
Facade Element	*Checklist Items*	*Possible Points*	*Fill in Points Awarded*	*Fill in Percentage*	*Circle Ranking*
Use of Technology in a School or School District	Items 1 through 6	55 points			1 2 3
The Necessary Infrastructure	Items 7 through 15	104 points			1 2 3
Viable Instructional Strategy	Items 16 through 20	41 points			1 2 3
Totals		200		100%	

Composite Score Form

Total Possible Points: 200	Your Composite Score: _____	Your Facade Rating: _____
175–200 points	Outstanding Technology Program	A Rating
125–175	Satisfactory Technology Program	B Rating
100–125	Modest Phase of the Technology Facade	C Rating
75–100	Moderate Phase of the Technology Facade	D Rating
< 75	Severe Phase of the Technology Facade	F Rating

Appendix 2.2

*Examples of Letter of Request to Conduct the Survey
and Letter of Endorsement/Approval*

Auburn Middle School
619 Court Street
Auburn, Alabama 36210

Reply to: Mr. John Neff, Chairman
Auburn Middle School Technology Committee
1217 Church Drive
Genoa, AL 36211
Home Phone: 555-1356
Fax: 555-9288

To: Mr. Donn Marcus, Principal
Auburn Middle School
619 Court Street
Auburn, AL 36210

Subject: Request to Conduct Annual Technology Survey

February 4, 2001

Dear Donn,

Our Technology Program provides all students with supervised, state-of-the-art instruction in the use of machines and equipment. As you know, each year the Technology Committee conducts a 20-question survey to gauge our progress toward our strategic technology plan. This year, we would like your permission to conduct the survey during the week of March 17, 2002. Your consent would allow us to complete the survey, analyze the results, and report our findings to your staff and the school board before dismissing for the summer.

We will do our very best to see that each survey is supervised and that good investigation practices are maintained at all times. To ensure that our technology program continues to address the demands of instruction, we would also like to meet with you and your staff some time in the week following the survey to hear first hand how the program satisfies or falls short of your instructional expectations.

Similar to last year and with your concurrence, we will conduct the survey with the assistance of your technology coordinator, Mr. John Templeton. John was a tremendous support over the last two years and was a major aid in identifying shortfalls in the program and possible solutions.

We sincerely hope that your staff will be as forthright with their comments and suggestions as they have in the past. Together, our instructional technology program and instructional curriculum will continue to grow while providing a new tool for teaching and learning at Auburn Middle School.

Please use the following endorsement to indicate your understanding and cooperation in this survey. It may be sent to my home address shown in the "Reply To" section of this letter, or faxed to the number indicated above.

Yours truly,

John Neff, Chairman

Letter of Endorsement/Approval   February 11, 2001

To: Mr. John Neff, Chairman
Auburn Middle School Technology Committee
1217 Church Drive
Genoa, AL 36211

Dear John,

I understand the nature of the technology survey to be conducted at Auburn Middle School and hereby grant approval to perform the survey during the week of March 17, 2002. We will meet with your survey team the following Thursday, March 27, per your request for a staff interview to discuss our technology program.

Teachers and administrative staff will be informed of the general nature of the survey and the requirements for completing the 20-question checklist.

It is also my understanding that teachers and staff will be debriefed of the results upon completion of the assessment portion of the survey. We look forward to the analysis and your recommendations regarding how our technology program could be improved. Rest assured you will continue to have our full support in this matter, and we sincerely appreciate all the efforts of your committee during the last several years. We have come a long way.

Signature: _Donn Marcus_ _____ Principal

Date: _February 11, 2002_ _____

THE USE OF TECHNOLOGY

> *The Technology Facade:* **"The use of technology** *in a school or school district without benefit of the necessary infrastructure to adequately support its use as a viable instructional strategy."*

Parts Two through Five, the remainder of this book, present in detail the specific elements of instructional technology that make up the Technology Facade. Each remaining chapter begins with Section I, which looks at a specific element in the Facade. Some chapters may discuss a single question, whereas others address several applicable items.

Each chapter then examines related Technology Facade Checklist questions in Section II by addressing the purpose of each question; that is, this section explains why that question was included in the checklist and why it is a determinant of the health of a school's technology program. Section II next offers a justification of the points awarded. Readers should pay particular attention to this portion of the chapters because points may be modified before application to reflect a particular school's strategic approach to technology planning and implementation. After the points are discussed, any extenuating issues related to the Checklist item and the number of points merited by the item are presented. The issues discussed here may be used to influence the points awarded. Finally, to address the true purpose of the Technology Facade Checklist, recommendations are made for increasing the points received. School and district leaders in technology should review this portion of each chapter to discover possible ways of enhancing their composite scores and thereby reducing the effects of the Technology Facade.

The use of technology is the first of three critical components of the Technology Facade. Its placement at the start of the checklist was not mere chance. Although only 63 of the possible 200 points reside in this first component, without a high score in this component, overcoming the Facade is all but impossible.

It is no secret that the Facade focuses predominantly on instructional technology and deals with the use of hardware, software, and networks to teach. Only the term *instructional technology* adequately defines the total process. To reduce the effects of the Technology Facade, the use of technology must include an understanding of (1) the range of available technologies for the classroom, (2) computer competencies and skills for teachers and students, and (3) various classifications of technologies.

■ ■ ■ ■ ■ ▬▬▬▬▬▬▬▬▬▬▬▬▬▬▬▬▬▬▬▬▬▬

CHAPTER 3

INSTRUCTIONAL TECHNOLOGIES FOR THE CLASSROOM

Section I: Classroom Technologies

The Technology Facade explores many technologies for the classroom. It is important to understand that instructional technology encompasses not only computer hardware and software, but also networking and communications, as well as calculators, audiovisual materials, and computer-assisted instruction. Recommendations for teachers are provided for each technology to help teachers *model* technology (i.e., use technology routinely as both a teaching and learning tool in the classroom), *demonstrate* technology (i.e., exhibit technology via classroom discussion), and *apply* technology (i.e., promote use of technology by students to augment their learning). It is suggested that the following pages be retained as a handy reference guide for hardware, software, and communications when discussing the gamut of technology available for classroom application. Figure 3.1 provides a ready index when searching for the particular technologies that follow.

  1. Calculators and graphing calculators
Category: Hardware. **Description:** Machines that automatically perform specified arithmetic operations and mathematical functions. Standard calculators typically do not handle alphabetic data, whereas graphing calculators visually display their results as charts, graphs, and diagrams. **Recommendation:** Demonstrate, Apply.

  2. Computer-assisted instruction
Category: Software. **Description:** Computer-assisted instruction that provides courseware applicable to individual lesson objectives or curriculum goals. Features include format for drill and practice, assessment, grading, tracking, and reporting. Teacher-made or -modified instruction is offered by

FIGURE 3.1   Reference Guide to the Most Common Instructional Technologies

1. Calculators and graphing calculators
2. Computer-assisted instruction
3. Databases
4. Desktop publishing
5. Drill-and-practice instructional media
6. Electronic mail
7. Digitized encyclopedias
8. Games instructional media
9. Groupware
10. Graphic presentation
11. Hypertext/hypermedia/hyperlinks
12. Internet
13. Listservs
14. MIDI interfaces
15. Multimedia computers
16. Music synthesizers
17. Newsgroups
18. Office productivity
19. Problem-solving instructional media
20. Simulation instructional media
21. Spreadsheet
22. Tutorial instructional media
23. Video (film, videotape, laser, DVD)
24. World Wide Web
25. Word processing

some packages, although the process can be time consuming, expensive, and technical. **Recommendation:** Demonstrate, Apply.

3. Databases

Category: Software. **Description:** A collection of data organized to allow rapid access; a computerized record-keeping system. A database is a system consisting of data, the hardware that physically stores that data, and the software that utilizes the hardware's file system in order to (1) store the data and (2) provide a standardized method for retrieving or changing the data. Traditional databases are organized by fields, records, and files. **Recommendation:** Model, Demonstrate.

4. Desktop publishing

Category: Software. **Description:** Use of a desktop computer to produce camera-ready copy for printing. Desktop publishing makes use of word-processing programs, page layout programs, and a printer. A scanner is used to integrate images, and draw or paint programs are used to create individualized artwork. **Recommendation:** Demonstrate, Apply.

5. Drill-and-practice instructional media

Category: Software. **Description:** Application that presents information or skills that are best mastered through repeated rehearsal. Software typically provides instructions to the learners, calls for frequent responses from the learner while providing continuous feedback, and modifies the lesson accordingly. Most drill-and-practice packages measure student performances, compare them with past personal or peer results, and advise the instructor on the necessary succeeding instruction. **Recommendation:** Demonstrate, Apply.

6. Electronic mail

Category: Communication. **Description:** Transmission of messages over networks. Most email systems include a rudimentary text editor for composing messages. Sent messages are stored in electronic form until the recipient fetches them. Emerging standards are making it possible for users on all systems to exchange messages. In recent years, the use of email has exploded. By some estimates, there are now 25 million email users sending 15 billion messages per year. **Recommendation:** Model, Demonstrate, Apply.

7. Digitized encyclopedias

Category: Software. **Description:** In CD-ROM or online format, digital encyclopedias provide background and supporting materials for numerous topics (usually more data than print versions offer). Alphabetical indexes, high-speed search engines, and hard copy output are featured options. Multimedia capabilities include animated graphics, recorded sounds, and video clip recordings, in addition to text, photographs, and drawings taken from the original print medium. Interactive encyclopedias are emerging as the newest format allowing readers to retrieve, manipulate, and classify information according to their own needs. **Recommendation:** Model, Demonstrate, Apply.

8. Games instructional media

Category: Software. **Description:** Software that teaches by guiding participants through a prescribed series of rules and procedures to achieve a goal (learning objective). Often based on competition, either individually or in teams. **Recommendation:** Demonstrate, Apply.

9. Groupware

Category: Software. **Description:** A class of software that helps groups of colleagues organize their activities. Typically, groupware supports the following operations: scheduling meetings and allocating resources, email, password protection for documents, electronic messaging and chats, and file distribution. **Recommendation:** Model, Apply.

10. Graphic presentation

Category: Software. **Description:** Tools that provide business and instructional graphics, charts, and diagrams used in a formal presentation setting. Predefined background, text formats, page layouts, and output options are integrated into user-friendly aides in presentation design. Contemporary packages infuse images, clip art, sound, and video in addition to hyperlinks to the Internet and action buttons for user-initiated movement through the presentation. **Recommendation:** Model, Demonstrate, Apply.

11. Hypertext/hypermedia/hyperlinks

Category: Software. **Description:** Linking of graphics, sound, and video elements in addition to text elements. The World Wide Web is an example of a hypermedia system because it supports graphical hyperlinks and links to sound and video files. **Recommendation:** Model, Apply.

12. Internet
Category: Software. **Description:** A global network connecting millions of computers. Each Internet computer, called a host, is independent. Its operators can choose which Internet services to use and which local services to make available to the global Internet community. As of 1999, the Internet has more than 200 million users worldwide, and that number is growing rapidly. More than 100 countries are linked into exchanges of data, news, and opinions. **Recommendation:** Model, Demonstrate, Apply.

13. Listservs
Category: Software. **Description:** An automatic mailing list server developed in 1986. When email is addressed to a listserv mailing list, it is automatically broadcast to everyone on the list. The result is similar to a newsgroup or forum, except that the messages are transmitted as email and are therefore available only to individuals on the list. **Recommendation:** Demonstrate, Apply.

14. MIDI interfaces
Category: Hardware. **Description:** Acronym for musical instrument digital interface, a standard adopted by the electronic music industry for controlling devices that emit music, such as synthesizers and sound cards. At minimum, a MIDI representation of a sound includes values for the note's pitch, length, and volume. **Recommendation:** Model.

15. Multimedia computers
Category: Hardware. **Description:** The use of computers to present text, graphics, video, animation, and sound in an integrated way. Until the mid-1990s, use of multimedia was rare due to the expensive hardware required. With increases in performance and decreases in price, multimedia is now commonplace. Nearly all PCs are capable of displaying video, though the resolution available depends on the power of the computer. **Recommendation:** Model, Demonstrate, Apply.

16. Music synthesizers
Category: Hardware. **Description:** Digitizer that translates analog sounds (voice, music, etc.) into a computer-readable electronic representation. Used in conjunction with a MIDI interface, a synthesizer combines with hardware technology to offer a wide range of performance-oriented algorithms to enhance music production and distribution. **Recommendation:** Demonstrate.

17. Newsgroups
Category: Software. **Description:** Unlike electronic mailing lists, newsgroups allow readers to choose which topics they want to read. They don't clutter the mailbox with unsolicited messages, and they are organized by topic. Messages are posted, and other people read and reply. Their messages, in turn, are added to the growing list. **Recommendation:** Demonstrate, Apply.

18. Office productivity

Category: Software. **Description:** Set of applications designed to work together. Typically includes word processing, spreadsheet, presentation graphics, and database programs. Some of the programs may be available separately, whereas others come only bundled with other programs. Microsoft Office, Corel Word Perfect Suite, and Lotus SmartSuite are the major business application suites that provide additional tools to move data from one application more easily into another. In addition, common functions such as spell-checking can be installed once and shared among all programs. **Recommendation:** Model, Demonstrate, Apply.

19. Problem-solving instructional media

Category: Software. **Description:** An intelligent mathematical engine that describes problems to the computer, develops solutions for unknown quantities, and visualizes the values in the problem. As a tool for education, problem-solving software provides an environment in which students can easily practice solving an unlimited number of problems, see the results in animated two-dimensional and three-dimensional visualizations, and receive as much or as little help from the computer as they require. The program allows students to explore more subject areas and in deeper detail than they could by any other means. **Recommendation:** Demonstrate, Apply.

20. Simulation instructional media

Category: Software. **Description:** The process of imitating a real phenomenon with a set of mathematical formulas. Advanced computer programs simulate weather conditions, chemical reactions, atomic reactions, even biological processes. In theory, any phenomena that can be reduced to mathematical data and equations can be simulated on a computer. In practice, however, simulation is extremely difficult because most natural phenomena are subject to an almost infinite number of influences. One of the tricks to developing useful simulations, therefore, is to determine which are the most important factors. **Recommendation:** Demonstrate, Apply.

21. Spreadsheet

Category: Software. **Description:** Program that creates and manipulates numerical data electronically. In a spreadsheet application, each value occupies a cell that can define the type of data, the interrelationships among cells (formulas), and the names of each cell (labels). Once cells have been defined along with the formulas for linking them together, data can be modified and values selected to see how all other values change accordingly (what-if scenarios). **Recommendation:** Demonstrate, Apply.

22. Tutorial instructional media

Category: Software. **Description:** An instructional, usually self-paced, lesson or program that guides the user through a sequence of steps and objectives. **Recommendation:** Model, Apply.

23. Video (film, videotape, laser, DVD)

Category: Hardware. **Description:** Refers to recording, manipulating, and displaying moving images, especially in a format that can be presented on a television or computer monitor. Video is recorded with a video recorder (camcorder), computer (digital camera), or some other device that captures full motion. **Recommendation:** Model, Apply.

24. World Wide Web

Category: Communications. **Description:** A system of Internet servers that support specially formatted documents. The documents are formatted in a language called HTML (HyperText Markup Language) that supports links to other documents as well as graphics, audio, and video files. The user moves from one document to another simply by clicking on hot spots. Not all Internet servers are part of the World Wide Web. **Recommendation:** Model, Demonstrate, Apply.

25. Word processing

Category: Software. **Description:** Creates, edits, and prints documents. To perform word processing requires a computer, a special program called a word processor, and a printer. A word processor stores documents electronically on a disk, displays them on a screen, modifies them, and prints the results on a printer. The great advantage of word processing over using a typewriter is that changes may be made without retyping the entire document. **Recommendation:** Model, Demonstrate, Apply.

An impressive list of possibilities for teaching and learning surrounds the Technology Facade. It is interesting to note that since the advent of instructional technology and the maturity of technology as a science, the pendulum has shifted from a focus predominantly on hardware to a focus on software. Communications technologies were hardly even mentioned until the mid 1990s, when the popularity of the Internet exploded.

In Section II, three questions address instructional technologies for the classroom. Checklist items 1, 2, and 3 specifically examine the school's technologies and their availability, location, and utilization.

Section II: Technology Facade
Checklist Items 1, 2, and 3

1. **Are the technologies in your school used by classroom teachers, or is the computer teacher the only educator who dispenses technology-related instruction? Select one.**

	Points Available	Points Awarded
Computer teacher only	1	
A few teachers use technology, but not regularly	3	
A few teachers use technology routinely	5	
Technology is routinely used by many classroom teachers	7	
Your Score (7 possible)	➡	

ITEM 1—THE TECHNOLOGIES IN YOUR SCHOOL

Purpose of the Question

The Checklist begins with an assessment of the general technology atmosphere in the school. Most schools employ a computer teacher. Unfortunately, most also depend on the computer teacher as their technology advocate. Visitors to the school readily discover the computer teacher surrounded by hardware and software, whereas the remainder of the staff seem to ignore technology altogether. Item 1 awards a maximum of 7 points to schools that attest to a broad use of technology by the majority of its classroom teachers.

Justification for Points Awarded

Computer teacher only (1 point).   If the computer teacher is the only user of technology, award one point; some may argue against awarding any points for this response. However, a teacher devoted to computer education at a minimum fosters an environment in which the Facade can be addressed.

A few teachers use technology, but not regularly (3 points).   For purposes of this checklist, "a few teachers" is 10 percent or less of the faculty. "Not regularly" is defined as two or fewer times during a semester or grading period.

A few teachers use technology routinely (5 points).   Teachers "routinely" use technology when they draw on the resources of the computer room or audiovisual library three to six times during a semester or grading period.

Technology is routinely used by many classroom teachers (7 points). "Many" classroom teachers would include a majority of the instructional staff; over half of the teachers use technology at least three to six times during a semester or grading period.

Issues to Consider When Assessing This Item

- Teachers shy away from technology that is not properly maintained and is in constant need of repair. They quickly lose confidence in undependable technology.
- Many teachers do not feel personally qualified to use the technology. They may not be adequately trained in its operation, maintenance, diagnosis, and repair.
- Many teachers have not been properly introduced to the various software programs that are available in the school. Also, they are not aware of how such packages can be integrated into their curricula.
- Time is always a problem. Teachers do not have the available time to learn the various technologies on their own.
- Many schools have not kept up with the advances in technology that make them easier to use. Software publishers, for example, now include CD-ROMs as integral components of their hard copy textbooks and reference materials.
- Unyielding school policies and procedures deter technology planning. For example, school requirements to schedule a computer lab four weeks in advance detract from the teacher's flexibility.
- Related to the issue of scheduling is the availability of technology in close proximity to the teacher's classroom. Rolling multimedia carts across the hallway or campus often results in doing without and using nontechnology work-arounds.
- Why should a teacher employ technology? What are the incentives? In subsequent items, the Checklist examines a school's program for recognizing teacher initiative with respect to technology. For now, understand that the lack of a formal program can be offset only by explicit expectations from school administrators.

Recommendations for Increasing the Points Awarded

To increase the points awarded for this first Checklist item, encourage teacher involvement in technology in the following manner:

1. Maintain all technology in good working order. Ensure that backup systems (whether they be overhead projectors, a spare videocassette recorder, or simply not scheduling a computer lab to capacity) are available to quickly replace unusable equipment with a minimum loss of valuable instructional time.

2. In-service training for teachers is a small price to pay for the potential dividends in the increased use of technology. Local colleges and universities, in addition to private training centers, offer a wide menu of training sessions that can be targeted to specific hardware or software applications. It is imperative to understand that training is only one piece of teacher preparation. In addition to specific hardware and software packages, teachers must also receive training in the integration of that technology into their curricula. Perhaps the best source of such preparation is a school of education for preservice teacher preparation.

3. A library of educational software tucked neatly inside the cabinets of a computer lab will not help eradicate the Technology Facade. An appropriate topic for an in-service program might be a session to familiarize teachers with the technology-based materials available in a school or district, followed by discussions on academic content areas. A more in-depth examination of software packages and how they meet national, state, and local standards for teaching content material is also recommended.

4. Unless the administration offers compensatory time for teachers to explore the uses of technology, it remains unlikely that a school will reduce the effects of the Facade. Finding time for teachers to explore technology tells them two things. First, that technology in the classroom is important, it will not go away, and the administration expects results. Second, that the school values teachers' time and is willing to meet them halfway in the pursuit of academic excellence.

5. Nothing impacts the Technology Facade more than outdated technology. Few factors squelch a teacher's enthusiasm faster than obsolete software, archaic audiovisual equipment, and outmoded computers, not to mention the effect this has on students. Schools face a constant uphill battle to maintain the status of their technology in light of how fast students upgrade their own personal systems. Schools fighting the Technology Facade cannot afford to find themselves behind in this continuing evolution.

6. Some schools post a weekly sign-up sheet on the door of the lab. Scheduling conflicts are resolved by the computer teacher, and all support equipment is found in the lab. Other schools require teachers to complete a scheduling form (in triplicate of course). One copy is retained by the teacher, the second goes to the computer teacher to resolve conflicting schedules, and the third is routed to the front office so the principal can schedule the technician's time should additional software be required or special projection equipment be necessary. Guess which school is more successful in its use of technology?

7. Teachers need access to technology in a timely manner. If a school purchases only one licensed copy of a popular laserdisc-based science program, then teachers must seek out the multimedia cart locked in the AV (audio-visual) closet. If the cart is available, it must be rolled down the hallway across to the middle school classroom area, and into the teacher's classroom. If the cart is missing, it is the teacher's responsibility to find it. Obviously, this is not conducive to the use of technology.

8. Increasing the number of points awarded in this first item is possible if teachers use technology that they personally develop. Such instructional materials are much more likely to address learning objectives that the teacher feels are important. The reward system does not necessarily need to be based on monetary incentives. Recognition during in-service programs, articles in the local school newspaper, paid attendance at local technology conferences and workshops, and compensatory time off are suitable substitutes for a larger paycheck.

2. Are the computer facilities in your school . . . ? Select one.

	Points Available	Points Awarded
Locked during unsupervised periods such as recess, study halls, lunch, and before and after school	0	
Available before and/or after school	3	
Available when there are no classes scheduled	5	
Open during recess, study halls, lunch, and before and after school	7	
Your Score (7 possible)	➡	

ITEM 2—COMPUTER FACILITIES

Purpose of the Question

Item 2 of the checklist is a key indicator of the Technology Facade. One of the first scenarios described in Chapter 1 was the pretense of a technology-competent school based solely on a visual walk-through of the building. Many computer facilities exist only for show; they have neither sum nor substance when it comes to providing a service to teachers and students. The evolution of instructional technology often begins with locked doors, systems bolted to computer furniture, and an unhealthy affection for computer security, sometimes to the point where teachers and students avoid what should be a valuable tool for teaching and learning.

Justification for Points Awarded

Locked during unsupervised periods such as recess, study halls, lunch, and before and after school (0 points). During the times when students are most available, technology is not. Recess, study halls, and lunch, as well as before- and after-school times, offer students the opportunity to use their free time for word processing, using educational software, or Internet research. No points are awarded even if there is a good reason for the lack of access, such as insufficient teachers to staff the open lab and supervise the participants.

Available before and/or after school (3 points). Points are conferred to schools that make their technology more available. However, busing often prohibits awarding additional points. Many students arrive at school immediately before first period, and for many students, the bus is the only means of transportation in the afternoon.

Available when there are no classes scheduled (5 points). The availability of computer facilities during the academic day when classes are not scheduled is an easy five points. A big caveat, however, is that these points are awarded only when a significant amount of time is reserved.

Open during recess, study halls, lunch, and before and after school (7 points). Teacher and student access to computer facilities throughout the day may be possible only for schools hosting both a computer classroom and a separate computer lab.

Issues to Consider When Assessing This Item

- Student access is vital to ensure that challenged (both fast and slow) learners have the opportunity to use available technology tools.
- A policy of priority-setting establishes precedence for computer classrooms and computer labs for teachers, students, and formal classes.
- Teachers, as well as students, benefit from access to technology during free periods and before and after school.
- To receive the maximum number of points for this question, schools probably need more than one facility, perhaps a computer classroom (for ongoing literacy training) and a separate computer lab not routinely scheduled for classroom presentations.
- Lab staff typically honors the same schedule as classroom teachers; therefore, the issues of supervision, responsibility, and compensation come into play when considering expanded hours of operation for computer classrooms and labs.

Recommendations for Increasing the Points Awarded

1. Challenged learners should be given priority to ensure they have fair opportunity to use technology. Special education teachers, in particular, should schedule sessions frequently in computer labs to teach, assess, and reteach computer competencies and skills important to a student's progress in this area. Gifted and talented programs should likewise use technology to a greater degree, providing enrichment activities for those students who more quickly master new subject material.

2. Establish a system of priorities for scheduling blocks of time for computer classrooms and computer labs that are not scheduled. Priorities should consider the needs of teachers, students, special classes, teacher and staff in-service training, student associations (e.g., school newspaper, computer club, etc.), and school administrators.

3. Teachers should have access to technology on demand. For some schools, the best method of ensuring teacher contact with computers, educational software, the Internet, electronic mail, and so on is to make them accessible from home. Many school districts supply complimentary email accounts, unlimited connectivity to the Internet, and even loaner systems.

4. To diminish the Technology Facade, schools should strive for both a computer classroom to conduct formal computer literacy training and a computer lab that is routinely available for students and teachers. The computer classroom should be scheduled by the computer teacher and made available to classroom teachers to present their technology-based lessons. The computer lab should be available to students and teachers on a drop-in basis to conduct personal research, explore individual content areas, and use available tools such as word processing, spreadsheets, database, and graphics preparation packages.

5. Expanding the hours of operation for computer classrooms and labs implies staffing considerations. Successful schools stagger staff hours so that the facilities are operational from 7:00 a.m. to 7:00 p.m. Obviously, at least two staff members are required, or an active and reliable volunteer program must be in place to accommodate 12-hour rotations. Shifts typically run from 7:00 a.m. to 11:00 a.m. with an hour for lunch, followed by an afternoon shift from 12:00 p.m. to 4:00 p.m. The second staff member will begin a daily schedule at 10:00 a.m. with lunch from 2:00 p.m. to 3:00 p.m., followed by a late afternoon/evening schedule from 3:00 p.m. to 7:00 p.m.

6. Since the availability and operation of computer facilities are particular to a school, reducing the effects of the Technology Facade is best served by surveying the school community to determine its preferences, restrictions, and associated issues. A survey may identify several additional issues regarding facility access that must be resolved.

3. School computers are located in our . . . : Select all that apply.

	Points Available	Points Awarded
Library	1	
Classrooms	3	
Computer Lab	3	
Your Score (7 possible)	➡	

ITEM 3—LOCATION OF COMPUTERS

Purpose of the Question

Technology typically finds its way into schools via the library, historically one of the few offices with its own recurring budget sufficient to explore technology. Libraries, as a rule, purchase the first few machines in hopes of digitizing their card catalog. Once in place, however, administrators find these machines are in great demand, often for activities totally unrelated to library science. Technology evolves in an atmosphere of competition and discord until the only agreeable solution is to relocate all computers to a single site—the computer laboratory.

Technology instruction, in turn, advances at a slower pace until it settles on the need to teach critical computer literacy skills such as keyboarding, word processing, electronic mail, spreadsheets, and, more recently, the World Wide Web. As still more teachers come to realize the possibilities of these tools, computers are finally introduced into the classroom. Item 3 accounts for this evolution of technology in schools, and awards up to 7 points for the presence of computers in the library, computer lab, and classrooms.

Justification for Points Awarded

Library (1 point).   Since computers usually begin in the library, minimal points are awarded, and only if those machines are used primarily for student research and exploration, not simply as an automated card catalog. There must be enough systems to support at least 10 percent of students who use the library at any one time during normal business hours. If the library typically serves 20 to 40 students during a normal morning class period, there must be at least two to four computers to receive the 1 point awarded for this response.

Classrooms (3 points).   To receive 3 points for this response, the number of computers located in classrooms must be able to support cooperative learning groups, remedial instruction, or discovery learning exercises. Although the composite number of systems varies depending on class size and teacher preference, points should not be awarded unless all students are able to participate in a simultaneous experience using technology. If a typical discovery learning exercise calls for 24 students to be divided into learning groups of six, there should be at least four computers in the classroom to secure the maximum number of points for this response.

Computer lab (3 points).   Computer labs are characteristically equipped with the most up-to-date hardware and software. In addition to providing a basic set of computer skills to students, the lab is often the showcase facility for dignitaries and visitors. To receive 3 points, a computer lab must provide enough machines to support any class conducted within its walls—one machine per student. Sharing computers, especially when presenting competency-based instruction, severely reduces the effectiveness of the technology.

Issues to Consider When Assessing This Item

- Replacement and reallocation usually begin with the usual succession of computer technology from the library to the computer lab and finally to the classroom, where equipment may be used for several years. As technology advances and upgrades provide new and faster hardware, outdated equipment is often relegated to the classroom.
- Teachers are the driving force for implementing technology-based curricula. Computers are virtually useless in a curriculum that has not first been modified to take advantage of technology. Educational magazines and technical journals are ready sources of ideas for the integration of technology into age-appropriate academic content, and should be evident in teacher lounges and school offices.
- Professional organizations are rapidly advancing the state of research regarding classroom technology, and revised academic standards are the resulting product. Many states are updating elementary, middle, and high school standards with learning objectives that demand more technology literacy from our teachers.
- Libraries, computer labs, or computer-equipped classrooms each deserve a place on the administrator's list of priorities when it comes to technology.
- Ninety-five percent of any group opposes change; the remaining 5 percent comprise the innovators. Computers in the hands of a few selected teachers can spark a revolution in technology, if you can determine who those innovators are.
- Computers in libraries offer access that might not otherwise be possible during the school day. The library is typically open from first period to

last period, and some schools provide students with designated library time for personal online research and study.

- Computers in classrooms have the obvious advantage of immediate access for convenient research, on-demand computer-based instruction, and unscheduled group activity. They provide ready access to classroom management software that assists teachers in lesson planning, student grading, and student tracking and reporting.
- Computer labs have significant advantages when conducting large-group presentations and shared learning opportunities, and they are most effective when limited technology resources are a concern.

Recommendations for Increasing the Points Awarded

1. Abandon or modify policies to encourage rather than discourage the use of technology. For example, although the library, classroom, and computer lab must be operated as separate entities, they are best managed as a single enterprise. Relocating obsolete, outdated equipment from the library to a teacher's classroom or from the computer lab to the faculty lounge is evidence that administrators do not take their commitment to the technology program seriously.

2. Do not hold a technology program hostage to the promises of a grant application. They are seldom successful, leaving few alternatives for acquiring the promised technology. Classroom teachers and their students are quick to become disillusioned with repeated broken promises pertaining to technology.

3. Do not schedule in-service training without offering the time for teachers to actually use the acquired skills. Once trained, teachers must apply what they have learned in a practical classroom environment as soon and as often as possible.

4. Do not expect a revolutionary change in teacher attitudes unless administrators take an active role in the technology program. Consider follow-on technical support to show your teachers that you value their time and the training they received—and that you expect tangible results.

5. Help teachers distinguish between using technology as a tool and using technology to support other learning objectives. Curriculum change is not a rapid process; integrating technology may take even longer.

6. Subscribe to several technology journals and place them strategically in teacher lounges and school offices. Accept only those publications that target age-appropriate materials for your particular school. A few of the more popular technology journals are presented in Table 3.1 along with each journal's focus, cost, Internet location, and email address.

TABLE 3.1 Instructional Technology Journals

PUBLICATION	TECHNICAL FOCUS	COST PER YEAR	INTERNET ADDRESS	EMAIL ADDRESS(ES) OR PHONE NUMBER
T.H.E. Journal	K–12	Free	www.thejournal.com	editorial@thejournal.com subscriptions@thejournal.com
ESchool News	K–12	$72	www.eschoolnews.org	k12-talkback@eschoolnews.com
Syllabus Magazine	K–12	Free	www.syllabus.com/syllmag.html	www.syllabus.com
International Journal of Educational Technology	Higher Education	Free	www.outreach.uiuc.edu/ijet	IJET@lists.ed.uiuc.edu
Journal of Technology Education	Higher Education	$12	http://scholar.lib.vt.edu/ejournals/JTE	—
American Journal of Education	Higher Education	$31	www.journals.uchicago.edu/AJE	aje@uchicago.edu
Technology & Learning	K–12	$30		1-800-607-4410
Educational Leadership	K–12	$49	www.ascd.org	member@ascd.org
From Now On	K–12	Free	www.fno.org	fromnowon@earthlink.net

7. Use an in-service session to introduce and discuss local, state, and national standards for technology. Teaching science, mathematics, language arts, and social studies using technology should become the goal once computers are actually available in the classroom.

8. Prioritize technology for the library, computer lab, and classroom, and do it across the school or district. Do not permit politics to enter into a decision regarding the placement of computers or the upgrade of technology. This admonition also applies to donated technology. Do not allow any organization, however well-meaning, to dictate the location of computers, access policies for particular student organizations, or the replacement cycle for outdated equipment.

9. Give the latest and greatest technology to your teacher–innovators. Make it clear to the rest of the faculty why this decision was made and how they too can be recognized as an innovator. Follow up with explicit expectations along with quantitative measures for success.

10. Locate computers in libraries to foster teacher and student access throughout the academic day. A policy concerning computer-related activities should be posted in a prominent location. For example, students wishing to surf the Internet are a lower priority than those trying to prepare a report using word processing. Well-advertised policies help the librarian decide which students should be using the limited resources.

11. Get computers into the classroom as quickly as possible. Teachers will not integrate technology unless it is readily available in their own classroom. Once installed, ensure that the computer has age-appropriate software for grade-specific academic content and contains user-friendly classroom management software to encourage teachers use it.

12. Schedule parent–teacher meetings, open house introductions, and senior citizen–parent training sessions in the computer lab to showcase your technology program. A computer lab presents an impressive "front door" for potential contributors to the technology program. Its effectiveness with large-group presentations makes the computer lab a logical choice for teacher in-service programs. Finally, if funding is an issue, a computer lab is an effective use of shared technology resources.

CHAPTER 4

COMPUTER COMPETENCIES AND SKILLS FOR TEACHERS AND STUDENTS

Section I: Computer Competencies and Skills

The National Council for Accreditation of Teacher Education (NCATE) is the official body for accrediting teacher preparation programs. The International Society for Technology in Education (ISTE) is the professional education organization that, together with NCATE, developed a set of de facto standards for accrediting programs in educational computing and technology teacher preparation.

> The ISTE Foundation Standards reflect professional studies in education that provide fundamental concepts and skills for applying information technology in educational settings. All candidates seeking initial certification or endorsements in teacher preparation programs should have opportunities to meet the educational technology foundations standards. (ISTE, 1998, para.1)

COMPUTER SKILLS AND THE FACULTY

The following technology standards are for *all teacher candidates seeking initial certification.* They consist of a list of technical skills and competencies to be acquired before a teacher is hired, and continuing through the first 5 years of classroom teaching and a lifetime of continuing professional development.

Standard for Basic Computer/Technology Operations and Concepts

Teachers will use computer systems to run educational software. They will access, generate, and manipulate data and publish results. They will operate hardware and software components of computer systems and apply basic

52

troubleshooting strategies as needed. Specifically, teachers must learn to do the following:

- Operate a multimedia computer system with related peripheral devices and successfully install and use a variety of software packages.
- Use terminology related to computers in written and oral communications.
- Describe and implement basic troubleshooting techniques for multimedia computer systems with related peripheral devices.
- Use imaging devices such as scanners, digital cameras, and video cameras with computer systems and software.
- Demonstrate uses of computers and technology in business, industry, and society to their students.

Standard for Personal and Professional Use of Technology

Teachers will apply tools to enhance their own professional growth and productivity. They will use technology in communicating, collaborating, conducting research, and solving problems. In addition, they will plan and participate in activities that encourage lifelong learning and promote the equitable, ethical, and legal use of computer/technology resources. Specifically, teachers must learn to do the following:

- Use productivity tools for word processing, database management, and spreadsheet applications.
- Apply productivity tools for creating multimedia presentations.
- Use computer-based technologies including telecommunications to access information and enhance personal and professional productivity.
- Use computers to support problem solving, data collection, information management, communications, presentations, and decision making.
- Demonstrate awareness of resources for adaptive assistive devices for students with special needs.
- Demonstrate knowledge of equity, ethics, legal, and human issues concerning use of computers and technology.
- Identify computer and related technology resources for facilitating lifelong learning and emerging roles of the learner and the educator.
- Observe and later participate in demonstrations and uses of broadcast instruction, audio/video conferencing, and other distance learning applications.

Standard for Application of Technology in Instruction

Teachers will apply computers and related technologies to support instruction in their grade level and subject areas. They must plan and deliver instructional units that integrate a variety of software, applications, and learning tools. Lessons developed must reflect effective grouping and assessment strategies for diverse populations. Specifically, teachers must learn to do the following:

- Explore, evaluate, and use technology resources, including computer applications, tools, educational software, and associated documentation.
- Describe current instructional principles, research, and appropriate assessment practices related to the use of computers and technology resources in the curriculum.
- Design, deliver, and assess student learning activities that integrate technology for a variety of learning strategies and diverse student populations.
- Design student learning activities that foster the equitable, ethical, and legal use of technology.
- Practice responsible, ethical, and legal use of technology, information, and software resources.

COMPUTER COMPETENCIES AND THE STUDENT

Assessing student competencies involves the seven categories of skills identified in this section. Each skill should be demonstrated by the prospective graduate based on his or her level of academic achievement. For example, although some competencies are common across elementary and middle school, the level of mastery deepens as the student advances to high school and post-secondary education. As ISTE explains,

> "Technology skills are developed by coordinated activities that support learning throughout a student's education. These skills are to be introduced, reinforced, and finally mastered, and thus, integrated into an individual's personal learning and social framework. They represent essential, realistic, and attainable goals for lifelong learning and a productive citizenry." (ISTE, 2000, p. xi)

Standard for Identifying Parts and Vocabulary of a Computer

Students must recognize the various components of technology available in the classroom. The corresponding competencies for this foundation are shown in the following list. Specifically, a student must be able to identify and use the following components:

Keyboard	Printer
Mouse	Video recorder
Monitor	Camcorder

Processor	Digital camera
Disk drive	Scanner
CD-ROM	Removable storage

Standard for Use and Care of Technology

A proper understanding of the care and operation of technology offers students a sense of stewardship for the high cost of hardware. The corresponding competencies for this foundation include

- Rules for safe handling of classroom technology
- Specific operational instructions and guidelines
- Respect for technology costs and expenses
- Care of disks, software, and storage media
- Ethics and social responsibilities of using technology

Standard for Keyboarding

Typing classes traditionally provided the necessary office skills to ensure successful employment at least in white-collar occupations. For the student of the twenty-first century, keyboarding has replaced the standard typewriter, and the mouse is becoming a necessary skill for producing the written word. The keyboard requires a student to learn how to

- Recognize alphanumeric keys
- Recognize the Return key
- Recognize all keys
- Acquire appropriate typing skills

Standard for Word Processing

Closely associated with keyboarding skills is the related competency of word processing, the most common of all computer applications. The corresponding competencies for this foundation include the ability to

- Create a document
- Type text with added graphics
- Save, edit, retrieve, and print documents
- Highlight/select text and cut, copy, or paste it
- Spell- and grammar-check documents
- Change font, style, size, and formatting options
- Insert page numbers, page and column breaks, and tab stops
- Create lists and outlines

Standard for Spreadsheet

Programs that create and manipulate numerical data electronically were among the first software packages that justified owning a personal computer. Now found in every office productivity groupware package, spreadsheets offer a range of competencies geared primarily to the middle school and older student. Students must be able to use spreadsheet functions to

- Highlight cells
- Enter text
- Work with formulas
- Adjust row and column height
- Format numbers
- Add graphics
- View page breaks
- Print worksheets
- Sort data
- Create charts
- Set displays, dates, and times
- Divide windows
- Lock/unlock cells

Standard for Paint/Draw and Graphics Presentation

Regardless of the platform, all state-of-the-art computers come with utility software that assists in the design and manipulation of graphics. Paint and Draw programs open graphic files, perform various modifications, and save results for use in word processing and web documents. Graphic presentation systems offer more sophisticated capabilities, including not only graphics design, but also classroom presentation features. The corresponding competencies for this foundation are identified in the following list. Students must be able to

- Create new images using basic graphic tools
- Draw shapes
- Select, add, and delete objects
- Resize objects
- Change fill and line patterns and line color
- Copy, paste, and duplicate objects
- Rotate and align objects
- Use a text box to insert text
- Group and ungroup objects
- Use paint tools
- Create slide shows and hard copy output

Standard for Multimedia Presentation

Combining many of the competencies from the previous foundations, multimedia presentations connect text, images, sounds, video, and hyperlinks in a way hardly imagined when the Internet was first established. Students will be expected to graduate from high school with at least a minimum set of the following skills:

- Harvest resources from the Internet
- Add and edit images
- Add sound
- Add video
- Add Internet links

As important as teacher and student skills are to the elimination of the Technology Facade, the proper application of these tools in pursuit of classroom teaching and learning is even more vital. Section II turns our attention to Technology Facade Checklist questions 4 and 5, which assess the breadth of technologies applied by classroom teachers.

Section II: Technology Facade Checklist Items 4 and 5

4. Do classroom teachers use technology for . . . ? Rate each separately.

	Points Available				Points Awarded
	Never	Seldom	Occasionally	Routinely	
Grading	0	1	3	5	
Lesson preparation	0	1	3	5	
Out-of-class assignments	0	1	3	5	
Professional development	0	1	3	5	
Your Score (20 possible)	➡	➡	➡	➡	

ITEM 4—TEACHERS' USE OF TECHNOLOGY

Purpose of the Question

Gradebook software often accounts for a teacher's first introduction to technology. And few teachers oppose the benefits that technology offers in the area of lesson preparation. Teachers also usually know the status of technology in the homes of their students; home-based technology opens the doors to out-of-class assignments and parental interaction. Finally, professional development is predicated on lifelong learning, and technology is one measure of teacher intention to remain current in state-of-the-art advancements in the field. A total of 20 points is available for this question.

Justification for Points Awarded

Grading (0, 1, 3, or 5 points).   Gradebook software includes features such as weighted assignments, calculation of letter grades, unlimited number of period divisions (e.g., semesters, quarters, final tests), attendance tracking, automated report generation, and lesson plan scheduling. Obviously, points are awarded only if teachers are using this tool, and a maximum of 5 points are available if the software is used every grading period.

Lesson preparation (0, 1, 3, or 5 points).   Educational software and electronic mail are excellent sources of new content material. The Internet, in particular, contains a growing wealth of resources appropriate for the classroom. It is hard to imagine teachers who would score a zero on this item; they would simply be missing out on a rich source of the latest information, ideas, and materials.

Out-of-class assignments (0, 1, 3, or 5 points).   Many students own home computers rivaling any technology available in their school. Out-of-class assignments expand the horizons of both teacher and student. Again, it hardly seems possible that teachers would not score at least three and possibly all five points.

Professional development (0, 1, 3, or 5 points).   Professional development for teachers involves six key domains: reading, writing, thinking, interacting, viewing, and demonstrating. Each of these domains is further enhanced by the technologically literate teacher. Reading expands to include online resources so vast that a trip to the local library pales in comparison. Writing, too, is improved with the technology of word processing and desktop publishing because electronic mail replaces traditional ways of contacting prospective publishers. Thinking is greatly enriched by new technologies that expose teachers to the latest research in science, math, social studies, and language arts. Viewing is the newest domain and characterizes learning outcomes resulting from visual stimulation; conference presentations and videoconferencing sessions are two examples. Demonstrating takes the teacher into the active role of learning and sharing, and technology provides the new forum for imparting professional knowledge via telecommunications, CD-ROM–based materials, and multimedia presentations.

Issues to Consider When Assessing This Item

- As teachers prepare lessons for the twenty-first century, they will increasingly choose existing resources, validating these materials against their own learning objectives and integrating the most promising pieces into a revised curriculum.
- Report cards are often generated by computer. "Cutting their teeth" on gradebook applications encourages teachers to develop an increasingly complex set of computer skills.
- Technology can be a tremendous boon to teachers who wish to expand communication with parents. Electronic mail and online web pages alert parents to classroom assignments, upcoming school and classroom events, and lapses in student performance.
- Out-of-class assignments offer cooperative learning opportunities that would otherwise go unrealized because of limited free time in a computer lab, inadequate numbers of computers in the classroom, or a lack of flexibility in scheduling technology resources.
- Preservice teacher preparation programs at 4-year universities and colleges of education are just beginning to groom their graduates in technology. A variety of teacher technology skills integrated into undergraduate programs include basic computer operations and concepts, personal and professional uses of technology, application of technology in instruction, theory of computer competency and the student, parts and vocabulary of a computer, the use and care of technology, keyboarding, office productivity tools, and multimedia presentations.

Recommendations for Increasing the Points Awarded

1. Ensure that classroom management software is found in the initial set of technology tools for teachers. Gradebook software, online research, out-of-class assignments, and professional development should be the first four in-service sessions. Familiarization with these tools immediately increases teacher interest in technology and builds confidence in its future.

2. Depend on the teacher–innovator to identify favorite Internet sites for new lesson materials. Table 4.1 offers a few sites targeting curriculum development and lesson design.

TABLE 4.1   Internet Sites Appropriate for Curriculum Development and Lesson Design

WEB ADDRESS	SOURCE TITLE	SITE CONTENTS
www.pbs.org/ teachersource	PBS [Public Broadcasting System] TeacherSource Page	Technology alliances with companies that support PBS TeacherSource's mission to serve pre-K–12 educators
school.discovery.com/ schrockguide	Kathy Schrock's Guide for Educators	Categorized list of sites on the Internet found to be useful for enhancing curriculum and teacher professional growth
www.geocities.com/ ~webwinds/k12/ projects.htm	Web Winds	K–12 projects, lesson plans, and interactive Web activities (with samples)
www.lessonplanspage .com	The Lesson Plans Page	Home to over 550 free lesson plans
LessonPlanz.com	Lesson Plans Search Index	Search or browse online lesson plans and resources for math, social studies, science, reading, writing, language arts, and thematic units
educate.si.edu/ut/ search_fs.html	Lesson plans section of the Smithsonian Center for Education and Museum Studies	Collection of classroom-ready lessons and activities that match the Smithsonian Institute's expertise to your classroom needs
www.teachersfirst. com/class.shtml	Classroom Resource Finder	Select among Classroom Resources or Lesson Plans. Grouped by subjects or search reviews color-coded by grade level: elementary, middle school, high school, AP, and advanced topics.

   3. Ensure that the trainer has practical experience (i.e., a reputation as a teacher) in developing technology-based learning objectives; integrating a broad spectrum of technologies (e.g., films, audio tapes, programmed texts, and laserdisc programs as well as computers); a commitment to student learning outcomes as the final assessment of success; and the proper appreciation for technology as a tool for learning, not simply as an end in itself.

4. Start a library of educational software selected by teacher committee, and provide opportunities to examine these materials during preparation periods.

5. Foster electronic collaboration via email among teachers in your school and other schools in your district, region, or state. Consider broadening the network to teachers sharing similar academic disciplines across the country or the world.

6. Train teachers to input, validate, and transfer grades during the report preparation period at the end of each academic term. Provide refresher training each reporting period to avoid frustration and mistakes.

7. Encourage teachers to communicate with parents using electronic mail and online web pages. Provide appropriate training and technical assistance to ensure success. Realize that email may not be available or even desirable by all parents, so it must not become the exclusive means of contacting parents. However, for some parents, reading an email message or clicking on a teacher's web site is the perfect solution for tracking their child's progress and staying informed about school events and activities.

8. Assign computer-based homework to students after surveying the class to determine the availability of home-based technology. It might be necessary to team students without home access with those that have such capabilities. Computer-based homework offers yet another opportunity to communicate with parents. A short description of the assignment, the technologies involved, and a request for their active participation make parents partners in the education of their children.

9. Encourage teacher development by offering technology-oriented opportunities for professional growth in the key domains of

- Reading: online journals, CD-ROM–based materials, access to the Internet
- Writing: word processing and desktop publishing
- Thinking: journal writing and electronic portfolios
- Interacting: electronic mail, newsgroups, and the Internet
- Viewing: graphics presentation software and audiovisual materials
- Demonstrating: participation in technology seminars, conferences, and workshops

10. Include technology as part of the interview process for prospective new teachers. Before hiring new staff, examine their preparation, understanding, experience, and personal philosophy regarding various technology skills and competencies, including basic computer operations, personal use of technology, technology in instruction, and technology and student learning.

5. **Is the computer teacher expected to have lesson plans with specific student learning objectives related to technology competencies? Select one.**

	Points Available	Points Awarded
Computer instruction is not based on lesson plans	0	
Lesson plans are not used. There are general goals for instruction, but no specific learning objectives	1	
Lesson plans contain generic technological competencies and general learning objectives	3	
Detailed lesson plans are used that reflect specific technological competencies expected of each student	7	
Your Score (7 possible)	➡	

ITEM 5—STUDENT LEARNING OBJECTIVES

Purpose of the Question

Technology is a relatively new curriculum area, especially when considering how long reading, writing, and arithmetic have existed and how many times they have undergone major revisions in philosophy and implementation. State and local education agencies revise their academic standards frequently, but technology standards have only recently been adopted in many states. Likewise, publishers have spent decades refining their text-based materials for the three R's. But informed textbooks that teach younger students to use the computer are still a rare find.

Because technology is so new, it understandably lags behind other subject areas when it comes to teacher-ready lesson planning aids. It remains the responsibility of the computer teacher to develop and refine lesson plans for instruction. This question considers the technology lesson plan—whether it exists and, if it does, whether it contains comprehensive learning objectives.

Justification for Points Awarded

Computer instruction is not based on lesson plans (0 points).   No points are awarded to a technology program that is not guided by lesson plans with specific learning goals and lesson objectives. Computer teachers have been permitted to instruct their students without a requisite agenda of competencies and skills to be mastered.

Lesson plans are not used. There are general goals for instruction, but no specific learning objectives (1 point).   Many computer teachers are able to produce a list of nonspecific topics for upcoming classes. They might include keyboarding function keys, spell-checking a document, using the printer, or inserting graphics into a presentation. Students cannot be expected to master content material that is ill-prepared, poorly sequenced, or presented in a catch-as-catch-can manner.

Lesson plans contain generic technological competencies and general learning objectives (3 points).   Three points are awarded to computer teachers who make a sincere effort to document the sequence of technology-based instruction with competencies and learning objectives, even if they cannot be considered specific in nature. For example, keyboarding is the generic description of a technology competency. However, if it is paired with a learning objective that balances specific computer skills such as home finger positioning, an introduction to the numeric keypad, and perhaps a look at the F1 through F12 function keys, points should be awarded.

Detailed lesson plans are used that reflect specific technological competencies expected of each student (7 points).   When the computer teacher's lesson plans contain the degree of specificity found in most other academic content areas, the full 7 points should be awarded. For this item, the focus is entirely on the computer teacher and the specific competencies taught in a dedicated computer literacy course.

Issues to Consider When Assessing This Item

- Although it is important that the school make a sincere effort to provide students with a technology-based curriculum, the computer teacher must remain the driving force in integrating and implementing a technology-based program.
- Many schools staff their computer labs with part-time instructors or nonteacher practitioners. Part-time instructors seldom have the same opportunities for in-service training and preparation time. As a result, they are often not held to the same standards for classroom readiness as full-time staff are.

- There may not be any state or local technology standards on which to base a lesson plan. At last count, only half the states have adopted such standards. Half still offer no guidance to their schools with respect to teaching technology. Although the more ambitious computer teachers take the initiative to use available standards from nearby states, many others do not.

- Research on the necessary computer skills required of students is sorely lacking. Although there is an increasing number of journals on the market, few offer the scholarly, qualitative, and quantitative research necessary for educators to know what works and what does not.

- Many states have not taken steps to formally certify their computer teachers. Only a handful of states offer a teaching certificate in instructional technology; most use math and science teachers to fill the demands of the computer classroom.

- In most schools, there is only one computer teacher who may be isolated when it comes to peer interaction and professional development. While the science teacher discusses academic content with a host of engaged faculty members, the computer teacher must be satisfied with the infrequent collaboration offered by districtwide training days, the occasional technology fair, or perhaps a parent or committee member that understands the difference between random access memory and a floppy disk drive.

Recommendations for Increasing the Points Awarded

1. Demand the same quality in lesson preparation, presentation, and student assessment from the computer teacher that is expected from every other teacher in the school—whether the computer teacher is part time or full time, certified or practitioner.

2. If a school must employ a part-time computer instructor, include a stipulation in the services contract that the individual must attend all teacher inservice programs (on a paid basis, of course). Also, if funding is available, include in the package a provision for compensated preparation time when the teacher can develop and refine lesson plans and learning objectives. Establish an understanding that the school has certain expectations for its computer classes. Make it clear that the computer teacher's time has equal value with the rest of the faculty. And demonstrate that the computer teacher is considered a professional educator on par with the rest of the faculty.

3. Become an advocate for state or local technology standards. If your state has already adopted such criteria, make them the topic of an upcoming inservice program. Help teachers understand the impact technology is having on the nation's schools. If your state does not have these standards yet, send an email to your state's department of education, and volunteer to serve on (or even initiate) a technology standards committee. Research how other states have constructed their standards, imitate the best, and modify the rest to suit the demands of your teachers and students.

4. Adopt a philosophy that encourages all teachers to explore the advantages of instructional technology in the classroom. An in-service program helps identify resources, makes the best use of limited funding, and fosters the unbridled enthusiasm of the faculty. Local area technology conferences, resident experts in teaching with technology, and after-school programs that train teachers, students, and parents should be considered.

5. Enroll teacher–innovators in a formal program of preparation in instructional technology. Stress the need for them to return as resource specialists for the staff in areas of applied technology research, academic standards, qualitative and quantitative foundations, and the assessment of student learning.

6. Develop a resource base of age-appropriate, technology-related audiovisual materials. Request assistance from local teacher stores. Ask them to forward catalogs, brochures, and special sales pertaining to technology materials.

7. Ensure that the computer teacher has the opportunity to interact with peers on classroom technology matters. Encourage attendance at districtwide training days and technology fairs, especially if they are offered to teachers free of charge.

BIBLIOGRAPHY

International Society for Technology in Education. "ISTE Recommended Foundations in Technology for All Teachers." 1998. Retrieved from http://www.iste.org/Standards/ncate
International Society for Technology in Education. *National Education Technology Standards for Students.* Eugene, OR: Author, 2000.

CHAPTER 5

A TAXONOMY OF INSTRUCTIONAL TECHNOLOGY

Section I: Technology Classifications

A *taxonomy* is "a classification in an ordered system that indicates natural relationships; a division into ordered groups or categories" (American Heritage Dictionary of the English Language, 1996). Benjamin Bloom created what is arguably the most famous classification for educators when he presented the Taxonomy of Educational Objectives (Bloom, Englehart, Furst, Hill, and Krathwohl, 1956). In his landmark exposition, Bloom developed a theory of six progressively complex steps of cognitive development. In that single manuscript, he offered classroom teachers a rubric for developing instructional objectives at increasingly advanced levels of higher-order thinking. Knowledge, comprehension, application, analysis, synthesis, and evaluation have taken their rightful place among the most practical theories of teaching and learning. But perhaps the most appealing aspect of Bloom's taxonomy is the subsequent research that resulted in a list of action verbs representing intellectual activity on each respective level. Table 5.1 presents a list of these verbs for the cognitive domain.

Likewise, Krathwohl (1964) took the lead to produce a parallel taxonomy explaining the development of attitudes, principles, codes, and human values. Five progressive stages constitute personal growth in the affective domain: receiving, responding, valuing, organization, and characterization. Table 5.2 offers some action verbs in this domain.

Finally, Kibler, Barker, and Miles (1970) completed the trilogy of taxonomies with the physical dimension of behavior as it develops from gross to fine movements and nonverbal to verbal activities. The categories here include gross body movements, finely coordinated movements, nonverbal communications sets, and speech-related behaviors. More action verbs are proposed in Table 5.3 for the psychomotor domain.

TABLE 5.1   The Cognitive Domain

TAXONOMY CLASSIFICATION	ACTION VERBS THAT REPRESENT INTELLECTUAL ACTIVITY ON THIS LEVEL
Knowledge	arrange, define, duplicate, label, list, memorize, name, order recognize, relate, recall, repeat, reproduce, state
Comprehension	classify, describe, discuss, explain, express, identify, indicate, locate, recognize, report, restate, review, select, translate
Application	apply, choose, demonstrate, dramatize, employ, illustrate, interpret, operate, practice, schedule, sketch, solve, use, write
Analysis	analyze, appraise, calculate, categorize, compare, contrast, criticize, differentiate, discriminate, distinguish, examine, experiment, question, test
Synthesis	arrange, assemble, collect, compose, construct, create, design, develop, formulate, manage, organize, plan, prepare, propose, set up, write
Evaluation	appraise, argue, assess, attach, choose, compare, defend, estimate, judge, predict, rate, core, select, support, value, evaluate

Source: Dembo, Myron. *Applying Educational Psychology,* 5th ed., p. 238. New York: Longman, 1994. Copyright © 1994, 1991, 1988 by Longman Publishing Group. Reprinted by permission.

TABLE 5.2   The Affective Domain

TAXONOMY CLASSIFICATION	ACTION VERBS THAT REPRESENT INTELLECTUAL ACTIVITY ON THIS LEVEL
Receiving	Differentiate, set apart, separate, accumulate, select, combine, listen, control
Responding	Comply, follow, commend, volunteer, discuss, practice, acclaim, augment
Valuing	Relinquish, specify, subsidize, help, support, protest, debate, argue
Organization	Theorize, abstract, compare, balance, define, formulate, organize
Characterization	Revise, change, complete, rate, manage, resolve

Source: Dembo, Myron. *Applying Educational Psychology,* 5th ed., p. 240. New York: Longman, 1994. Copyright © 1994, 1991, 1988 by Longman Publishing Group. Reprinted by permission.

TABLE 5.3 The Psychomotor Domain

TAXONOMY CLASSIFICATION	ACTION VERBS THAT REPRESENT INTELLECTUAL ACTIVITY ON THIS LEVEL
Gross body movements	Throw, run, swim, walk, etc.
Finely coordinated movements	Type, tune an instrument, use workshop tools, drive a car, etc.
Nonverbal communications sets	Use sign language, mime, use body language, etc.
Speech-related behaviors	Produce vowel sounds, recite a poem, speak comprehensively, transmit a verbal message, etc.

Source: Dembo, Myron. *Applying Educational Psychology,* 5th ed., p. 241. New York: Longman, 1994. Copyright © 1994, 1991, 1988 by Longman Publishing Group. Reprinted by permission.

Together, these taxonomies for cognitive learning, social interaction, and physical development are the recognized building blocks for writing lesson plans, creating measurable learning objectives, and evaluating results. How does a taxonomy work? Educators have developed a number of schemes for classifying learning skills. These schemes provide distinctions that are useful in organizing and creating learning objectives. They help in instruction and evaluation. Each scheme follows a similar format: from simple to complex, first to last, and general to specific.

THE TAXONOMY FOR INSTRUCTIONAL TECHNOLOGY

The literature has yet to adopt a taxonomy for technology, even though many educators have already come to accept teaching with technology as the newest and perhaps most important teaching strategy ever to hit the classroom. An accepted taxonomy—considered, contemplated, and adopted—suggests a new perspective for viewing technology and the spectrum of capabilities that actually produce learning. Of course, the very nature of a taxonomy reduces in scope whatever is being categorized because of its tendency to artificially place items into all-too-convenient pockets. However, the benefits for teachers who understand the advantage of sequential arrangement greatly outweigh such minor obstacles.

The technology domain proposed in Table 5.4 includes six levels that progressively increase in complexity from literacy to communications, decision

TABLE 5.4   The Technology Domain

TAXONOMY CLASSIFICATION	ACTIONS THAT REPRESENT INTELLECTUAL ACTIVITY ON THIS LEVEL
Literacy: understanding technology and its components	Apply computer terminology in oral and written communication
	Consider the various uses of computers and technology in business, industry, and society
	Master keyboarding and clicking and dragging objects
	Use web-based search engines
	Download information via file transfer protocol
	Operate input and output devices
	Duplicate solutions to routine hardware and software problems
Communications: sharing ideas, working collaboratively, and forming relationships using technology	Use technology tools for individual writing and personal communications
	Participate in demonstrations of distance learning applications, broadcast instruction, and audio/videoconferencing
	Share information electronically among students and teachers
	Value work conducted cooperatively and collaboratively with technology
	Respond to opportunities for sharing electronic information
	Communicate interpersonally using electronic mail
	Interact with the electronic community via chat rooms
	Subscribe to online newsgroups
	Access remote information via telecommunications
Decision Making: using technology in new and concrete situations	Apply electronic tools for research, information analysis, and problem solving
	Design effective instruction
	Evaluate the accuracy, relevance, and bias of electronic information sources
	Formulate new ideas with the help of brainstorming software
	Prepare an electronic spreadsheet
	Create calendars, address books, and class schedules
	Conduct research that enhances learning

(continued)

TABLE 5.4   Continued

TAXONOMY CLASSIFICATION	ACTIONS THAT REPRESENT INTELLECTUAL ACTIVITY ON THIS LEVEL
Instruction: breaking down technology-based instructional material into its components	Teach, differentiate, and discriminate using technology
	Appraise educational software for its pedagogical strengths
	Support learning goals by choosing developmentally appropriate multimedia resources
	Formulate a collegial environment for teaching and learning using technology-based tools
	Theorize instructional opportunities that might be adaptive to diverse learners
	Integrate technology into student guidance, career awareness, and student support activities
	Create teacher and student web-based materials
	Create text-based materials using technology
	Create visual-based classroom presentations
Integration: reassembling technology-based instruction to create new materials	Assimilate technology into a personal learning style
	Facilitate lifelong learning by constructing a personal schemata for using technology
	Address personal skill deficits using technology
	Explain the many applications of office productivity tools
	Consider the consequences of inappropriate uses of technology
	Enhance personal productivity with technology
Society: judging the value of technology	Support copyright and fair use laws for using technology
	Debate the issues surrounding legal/ethical behavior when using technology
	Argue and assess the historical evolution of technology and predict its probable future roles in society
	Rate the promises for using information technology to solve real-world problems
	Judge the responsible uses and abuses of technology

making, instruction, integration, and acculturation. The scale of six interconnected levels offers a new taxonomy for creating technology-related learning objectives and technology-based student learning. Can a taxonomy specifically addressing instructional technology advance the discipline of educational psychology and take its rightful place with the more widely accepted theories of teaching and learning?

Level One: Technology for Literacy

Literacy is defined as the minimum level of competency expected of teachers and students with respect to computers, educational programs, office productivity software, and the Internet. This first rung on the ladder of taxonomy establishes the most fundamental literacies for the technological learner. At this lowest level of intellectual activity, the educator proposes learning objectives steeped in computer skills that are likely to become mandatory in the foreseeable future before high school students are permitted to graduate or preservice teachers are awarded their certification as classroom instructors.

Here are two typical learning objectives grounded in Literacy:

After reviewing a list of selected computer terms, the student will label each of the respective pieces of computer hardware within 5 minutes.

Given a series of three keyboard exercises, students will create a word processing document for each exercise without syntax or grammatical error.

Literacy concerns an awareness of technology as well as the recall, consideration, and use of a wide range of material. All that is required here is the bringing to mind of appropriate information about technology in a timely manner.

Level Two: Technology for Communication

Level two is defined as the ability to employ technology for interaction. Effective uses include technology for written and oral communication, the professional exchange of information, and interpersonal collaboration. These skills may be evidenced by sharing information in written form (word processing, desktop publishing), by participating in and interpreting interpersonal dialog (via newsgroups, listservs, and chat rooms), and by responding to directed interchange (electronic mail).

Some example learning objectives in communications might include the following:

Using electronic mail, the student will subscribe to a science-related listserv and participate by initiating at least two original messages and replying to another four posted exchanges during the first 2 weeks of the semester.

Students will use the course-provided chat room at least weekly during the grading period to discuss the assigned readings with fellow classmates.

Communications goes one step beyond simple literacy, that is, the mere recall of important material. It requires active participation on the part of the learner and represents the lowest level of technical understanding.

Level Three: Technology for Decision Making

Decision making refers to the ability to use technology in new and concrete situations, including those of the previous two levels. Decision-making skills often begin with a teacher's need for classroom management. Helping students learn via technology includes such important tools as spreadsheets, brainstorming software, statistical analysis packages, and gradebook programs. Here is an example objective that reflects this level's strength.

After recording the quantitative results of a 2-week observation period, students will capture the resulting weather data in electronic format and use the "what-if" features of spreadsheets to forecast the next day's weather.

Learning outcomes at the decision-making level require greater understanding; the teacher is concerned for the first time with the merits of various technologies as tools for learning.

Level Four: Technology for Instruction

Technology is a potent tool for exploring academic subjects. At this level, learning outcomes center around identifying instructional materials, analyzing their component parts, integrating these components, and understanding the organizational principles involved in their application.

Teachers are expected to have a firm grasp of their academic discipline. The taxonomy continues to expand these expectations, however, with the incorporation of technology-based instruction, including printed materials, audiovisual multimedia, and web-based materials, in addition to the more traditional category of educational software. Examine a few learning objectives that demonstrate technology for instruction:

Students will locate four Internet sites concerning the Holocaust and select the site that best reflects their feelings and emotions about the Nazis' "final solution."

Using the computer lab, students will create a 5-page portfolio using word processing and graphics presentation software depicting the most important scenes of the Holocaust gathered from online material.

Prospective college applicants will use the resources of CD-ROM catalogs to research and identify at least three potential colleges based on area of the country, programs desired/offered, cost and financial assistance opportunities, and reputation and personal interest.

Level Five: Technology for Integration

Technology for integration acts on the component parts of content material and reassembles them for better learner understanding. For example, the Internet often presents site after site of relevant, but often disjointed, material. Using text-based technology, the teacher captures online text, only an image or two, and perhaps a few hyperlinks to bring together a lesson that is specific to the needs of the logical learner. Visual-based technology lessons appeal to the learning styles of the visual/spatial learner, while web-based instruction focuses on the strengths of interpersonal intelligence. Howard Gardner would be proud: in 1993 and again in 1999, Gardner submitted the idea that there is not a single "intelligence," but rather seven kinds of intelligence: visual/spatial, musical, verbal, logical/mathematical, interpersonal, intrapersonal, and body/kinesthetic. Teachers, using various technologies to present instruction in a variety of formats, select the ones that best fit the individual student. Example learning objectives at the integration level are as follows:

> Using a teacher-made workbook created from online resources, the students will explore the possible theories of dinosaur extinction, select their favorite theory, and prepare a grammatically correct essay defending one of the theories.

> Using a visual-based classroom presentation, students will review the skeleton of the human body and correctly identify 8 out of 10 major bones.

> Students will create their own Web page with the following minimum elements: photo digital image, email address, personal interests, and books read this semester.

Level-five technology integration moves the individual from user to advocate. A true proponent seeks to improve education by concentrating on the strengths of technology and shunning any weaknesses. Teachers must demonstrate and model technology—demonstrate when the situation does not permit a hands-on approach to learning the task, and model when the students must apply the lesson to the real-world environment in which they will find themselves. Outcomes here represent the highest level of understanding necessary for classroom learning.

Level Six: Technology in Society

Many social issues surface when considering the responsible use of technology. Multicultural issues, for example, include the increasing disparity of computer access between the wealthy and poor; the availability of information between the computer "haves" and "have-nots"; copyright and fair use laws and their impact; censorship on the Internet; and legal and ethical behavior when using information and technology. Technology in society concerns itself with the ability to judge the value of technology. Here is an example learning objective:

> Students will be provided copies of recent publications, journals, and newspapers. They will locate an article that reflects the legal/ethical use of technology and prepare a grammatically correct, 3-page minimum, double-spaced report defending or criticizing the premise of the work.

Taxonomies are a tool. Research has borne out that learning objectives consciously prepared produce successful learning outcomes. They do a better job of matching teaching strategies with student learning. It is time that technology join the pedagogical debate that has shaped this research base.

Literacy, communication, decision making, instruction, integration, and society offer a perspective for immersing technology into classroom teaching. The sooner we adopt a taxonomy for instructional technology and begin to rely on a new directory of action verbs to classify our technology-based learning objectives, the sooner we will ensure that technology matures into a successful teaching and learning strategy in its own right.

Section II discusses item 6 of the Checklist. Classifying technology use in the classroom is so important that this question offers a significant number of points toward reducing the Technology Facade.

Section II: Technology Facade Checklist Item 6

6. **Does the software found on your computers reflect current classroom curriculum? Select one.**

	Points Available	Points Awarded
Computer software is available, but its selection was not based on teacher input and seldom reflects actual classroom content	1	
Computer software was recently purchased but is not readily available for teachers and students to use	3	
Computer software selection was based on teacher input and its use on current curriculum objectives	5	
Computer software versions are current, software selection is based on teacher input, and the software is routinely used by teachers and students	7	
Your Score (7 possible)	➡	

ITEM 6—SOFTWARE AND THE CURRICULUM

Purpose of the Question

Successful use of computers often depends on current educational software on lab and classroom computers. Many schools provide teachers only with software that comes standard with newly purchased systems. To be a potent learning tool, educational software should be selected by the classroom teacher after careful consideration of established learning objectives. This item examines the various aspects of educational software: how it is selected, purchased, and ultimately used by the classroom teacher.

Justification for Points Awarded

Computer software is available, but its selection was not based on teacher input and seldom reflects classroom content (1 point). One point is awarded for educational software found on computers in the lab or classroom. Additional points are withheld if these packages are not selected by classroom teachers or if the software is purchased without regard for curriculum objectives.

Computer software was recently purchased but is not readily available for teachers and students to use (3 points). Educational software must be an on-demand resource. Showcasing a library of dusty software is like bringing a tour of prospective parents through an empty computer lab in the middle of the school day. Points are awarded only if software is available and both teachers and students are encouraged to use it.

Computer software selection was based on teacher input and its use on current curriculum objectives (5 points).   Award five points to schools that have an active selection committee for hardware and software. To receive the maximum number of points, schools must ensure that the software meets documented classroom learning objectives.

Computer software versions are current, software selection is based on teacher input, and the software is routinely used by teachers and students (7 points).   All three conditions must be present to receive the full 7 points. Software over 4 years old is highly suspect and must be reevaluated often to ensure it remains current. "Based on teacher input" is not evidenced unless the school has a formal process for teacher input; a simple survey of "select" or "do not select" is not sufficient. Finally, enough copies of the software must be available so that teachers will routinely use the packages for classroom application. Some means of inventory management and usage statistics is recommended to track software use.

Issues to Consider When Assessing This Item

- Software packages remain effective classroom tools as long as they meet lesson goals and result in student learning. Unlike hardware, software does not need to be replaced unless learning objectives change.
- Software costs depend on the source of the software, the scope of its content coverage, and the degree of support required for implementation.
- Finding satisfactory software is a challenge. There is a tendency to alter learning objectives to match available software rather than insisting on software that meets the demands of the lesson. Possible sources of software include professional associations, reputable vendors, and the Internet.
- Software is cheaper when purchased with a new system, especially office productivity tools such as word processors, spreadsheets, and database applications and software utilities including paint and draw programs, file compression, and clip art.
- Technology committees tend to concentrate on the more visible aspects of technology. Software packaging often "oversells" academic content and practical classroom application.
- Matching educational software to specific learning objectives assumes detailed lesson plans.

- Software is categorized as drill-and-practice, tutorials, and simulation. Classroom curriculum, however, is evolving toward integrated thematic units and the exploration of an applicable taxonomy for the technological domain.

Recommendations for Increasing the Points Awarded

1. Do not replace educational software packages simply because they are old or newer, more attractive packages appear on the market. Rather, evaluate software periodically to determine whether it still meets lesson goals and promotes student learning.

2. Include a review of available educational software and other instructional technologies during routine scheduled lesson rewrites.

3. During the selection process, consider a number of available software sources. Do not summarily dismiss shareware and freeware packages. Determine the extent of content coverage; software varies in quality and quantity of lesson goals addressed. Finally, take into account the sophistication of the teaching staff and the amount of technical support required following implementation.

4. Never shrink from important learning objectives because software is not available. Insist that it meet the demands of the lesson, or find another technology.

5. Make the technology committee responsible for keeping the instructional staff current on computer resources. In-service programs, faculty newsletters, journal articles, and in-school reviews are excellent ways to remain current on the rapidly changing venue of educational software.

6. Purchase software packages along with new computer systems. Include office productivity tools, system utilities, and instructional applications, and negotiate for the best prices as part of a package deal.

7. Ensure that the school's software selection team includes teachers. Then prepare them to evaluate potential software packages as teaching and learning tools.

8. Teachers must prepare detailed lesson plans before matching prospective software with current classroom curriculum. A valid evaluation plan correlates the strengths of proposed software to specific learning objectives.

9. Do not be taken in by slick software packaging. Reputable vendors offer free demonstration versions, an evaluation period during which rejected materials may be returned, and free technical support. Also, request a list of phone numbers or email addresses of satisfied customers. It may be a biased sample, but pointed questions often uncover issues and concerns that may be important to the purchase decision.

10. Consider educational technologies that integrate curricular areas as complete thematic units. Select publishers that offer accompanying workbooks or CD-ROM exercises, detailed lesson plans, prepared student assessments, and online resources such as Internet web sites for students to explore.

BIBLIOGRAPHY

American Heritage Dictionary of the English Language, 3rd ed. Boston: Houghton Mifflin Company, 1996.

Bloom, Benjamin S., Englehart, M. B., Furst, E. J., Hill, W. H., and Krathwohl, D. L. *Taxonomy of Educational Objectives. The Classifications of Educational Goals. Handbook I.* New York: Longman, 1956.

Dembo, Myron. *Applying Educational Psychology,* 5th ed. New York: Longman, 1994.

Gardner, Howard. *Frames of Mind: The Theory of Multiple Intelligences.* New York: Basic Books, 1993.

Gardner, Howard. *Intelligence Reframed: Multiple Intelligences for the 21st Century.* New York: Basic Books, 1999.

Kibler, R. J., Barker, L. L., and Miles, D. T. *Behavioral Objectives and Instruction.* Boston: Allyn & Bacon, 1970.

Krathwohl, D. L., Bloom, Benjamin S., and Masia, B. B. *Taxonomy of Educational Objectives. The Classifications of Educational Goals. Handbook II.* New York: David McKay Co., 1964.

Tomei, Lawrence A. "Using a Taxonomy for the Technology Domain." Pennsylvania Association of Colleges for Teacher Education. Monograph, in publication winter 2001.

■ ■ ■ ■ ■

THE NECESSARY INFRASTRUCTURE

> *The Technology Facade: "The use of technology in a school or school district without benefit of **the necessary infrastructure** to adequately support its use as a viable instructional strategy."*

The necessary infrastructure is composed of people, money, and resources. Each element is brought to bear in just the right mix to promote the integration of technology into schools. The infrastructure contributes over half of the possible points toward overcoming the Technology Facade. Yet it remains by far the most neglected of the elements, with negative effects on the long-term success of teaching and learning.

Business administration textbooks have long explained that, to be considered a true supervisor, a manager must control at least two of these three components: people, money, and resources. This also applies to the management of instructional technology.

PEOPLE

A true manager is responsible for hiring, firing, and rewarding employees. In education, people comprise the most complex element. Chapter 1 introduced

—students, parents, teachers, administrators, community
—who bring to the table their own agendas for integrating
classroom. A manager must effectively deal with all these
hat technology is effectively administered.

MONEY

The true manager controls fiscal planning and execution. Costs for information technology are more readily understood when viewed from the perspective of a balance sheet. "Hard" costs, for example, consist of the capital investment in computer hardware, software, and networking; installation costs for classrooms and computer laboratory; recurring hardware and software upgrades; and support personnel for installation, repair, and maintenance. "Soft" costs are much more difficult to quantify and include the less tangible aspects of teaching, such as renovation costs for computer classrooms and labs; instructor training time and professional development; and technology literacy in academic content areas. A manager must effectively control other aspects of funding as well, including technology-related operations and maintenance, budgeting, accounts receivable and payable, and payroll.

RESOURCES

The manager directs a vast array of resources needed to ensure that the teaching mission is accomplished with a minimum of interruption. Since educators first began using computers in the classroom, they have tried to assess whether educational technology makes a significant impact on student achievement. Unfortunately, technology cannot be treated as a single independent variable. Rather, it is composed of many interrelated and synergistic elements. Incentives and reward systems, public relations, professional development, in-service programs, community resources, legal issues, community involvement, and fair access concerns are only a few of the critical resources that lend themselves to this issue.

Any manager who does not directly control at least two of these three elements is not truly a manager. The manager of instructional technology may be called a principal, superintendent, or district administrator, but the designation is in name only. To be a true manager, an individual must make people decisions, money decisions, and resource decisions. Part Three explores these three key elements and offers many suggestions on how they can be effectively managed.

CHAPTER 6

THE PEOPLE OF THE TECHNOLOGY FACADE

Section I: Who Is Involved with the Technology Facade?

Who are the key players in education, and how do they impact the Technology Facade? As the list grows, it mirrors the increasing impact of technology as it expands to touch the educational lives of so many individuals. The following examination offers a working definition of these constituents and their impact on the Technology Facade.

STUDENTS

To compete successfully in the workplaces of tomorrow, students must become comfortable and competent users of technology. Schools that undertake these kinds of innovative programs often find themselves thinking differently about technology than they have in the past. Instead of viewing technological literacy as an end in itself, and instead of organizing computer classes in self-contained labs, schools begin thinking about how to integrate technology into an overall instructional program and across subject areas.

Students are the primary consumers of instructional technology in the classroom. Throughout the United States, over 46 million students in grades K–12 use computers, educational software, and Internet connections (NCES, 2000).

Impact on the Technology Facade: question 20. In their special capacity as customers of classroom technology, students contribute to the final score of the Technology Facade Checklist with virtually every question. Question 20, however, most directly affects the final composite score; here, students describe their experiences with the technology and its relevance to daily learning.

TEACHERS

Ultimately, the effective use of technology depends on the knowledge and skills of the classroom teacher; without question, the person with the greatest impact on the learning environment. Yet the need to prepare teachers and provide them with continuing technical support and professional development often receives lower priority than hardware acquisition and infrastructure renovations, as schools seek the most visible expressions of their technology program.

Teachers are the principal dispensers of instructional technology in the classroom. Throughout the United States, over 2.8 million teachers of grades K–12 are responsible for the advancement of technology in support of learning. Yet the typical teacher averages less than 12 hours of technology training in preparation for this important teaching strategy (NCES, 2000).

Impact on the Technology Facade: questions 4, 5, 8, 17, and 18.   As expected, many teacher-focused questions contribute to the final score of the Checklist. Question 4 offers four areas in which teachers should model the use of technology for their students. Question 5 alludes to expectations that teachers evidence technology-based competencies in their curriculum. A component of question 8 determines whether teachers are included in the planning of technology development. Question 17 determines whether text, visual, and web-based materials are prepared by teachers. And question 18 addresses learning objectives and technology-based resources.

CURRICULUM DESIGNERS

Curriculum designers support the integration of technology into the curriculum. Their responsibilities include assisting teachers in lesson design, professional development, student assessment, and collegial sharing of ideas. In addition, they support classroom activities via infusion of multimedia, gathering of technology resources, and technical support.

Curriculum designers prepare instructional programs. Research indicates that over 95 percent of school districts across the United States employ at least one full-time curriculum designer (NCES, 2000). An emphasis on local, state, and national standards typically guides their efforts. The standards for technology are changing fast. States are modifying their curricula to include such technologies as graphing calculators (math), collaborative reading software (language arts), laserdisc explorations (science and social studies), electronic communications (English/foreign languages), and office productivity software (all content areas).

Impact on the Technology Facade: questions 6 and 16.   The curriculum designer concentrates on two questions. Question 16 emphasizes scope and sequence. More often than not, schools shy away from specific grade-appropriate, technology-based requirements. To a somewhat lesser degree, question 6 is also a responsibility of the curriculum designer as previously used software rapidly becomes obsolete and ineffective.

TECHNOLOGY COORDINATORS

The role of the technology coordinator is relatively new in the scheme of district and school plant operations. Often their responsibilities include both classroom and computer lab tasks. Districts are still unclear about whether their technology coordinators should be certificated teachers or information systems professionals.

Although 98 percent of the districts polled in a recent nationwide survey responded that they have a technology coordinator assigned, the details are not quite as optimistic. For example, whereas only 2 percent of the schools surveyed claimed to do without a technology coordinator, only 30 percent employ their coordinators full time (NCES, 2000). The remainder of the schools placed the burden on part-time employees who are often shared among several school plants, or on overextended district staff members and overworked classroom teachers. The roles and responsibilities of the coordinator continue to reflect an uncertain opinion regarding technology. Most technology coordinators have the following duties and responsibilities:

- Technology maintenance, including setup of hardware, installation of software, software and hardware maintenance, network management, upgrades, management of the inventory database, and coordination of district resources.
- Leadership in the development and implementation of the Technology Plan and membership on the school or district Technology Committee.
- In-service help to staff on software and hardware issues, including classroom visitations on request and demonstrations to teachers and pupils.
- Consultant to teachers, principals, and site staff regarding the purchase and use of computers and other high-technology electronic devices.
- Effective role modeling for use of instructional technology.
- Maintenance of site equipment, software, and resources, and record keeping for these assets.
- Setup and installation of new equipment and software.
- Basic troubleshooting and maintenance work.
- Other duties as required.

Impact on the Technology Facade: questions 10 and 15.   Question 10 applies to the technology coordinator, along with a computer teacher and technician. In the Checklist, schools are awarded additional points against the Technology Facade for full-time coordinators. Question 15 also falls under the purview of the coordinator, who should become an advocate for replacing outdated technology and obsolete educational software.

BUSINESS MANAGER

The business manager deals on a daily basis with many aspects particular to technology. The business manager sees buildings, curriculum, personnel, utilities, grants, equipment, resources, and travel as the ingredients in a smorgasbord of normal operations. It makes perfect sense for this key player to be involved heavily to ensure the sensible integration of technology.

One of the most visible noncertificated professionals in education, the business manager often holds the purse strings of the school. Responsibilities encompass accounting, auditing, debt management, activity funds, and—most important for purposes of reducing the effects of the Technology Facade—budgeting. Along with budgeting and fiscal planning often come the charge as keeper of the strategic technology plan.

Impact on the Technology Facade: questions 11 and 13.   Question 11 is certainly one of the most penetrating inquiries on the Checklist. Only when technology appears as a recurring, separate line item in a school or district budget can a school truly be free from the effects of the Technology Facade. And only the business manager can make that happen. In addition, question 13 is extremely important for this key player. A viable instructional technology program must include a comprehensive technology plan, revised and referenced often.

PARENTS

A strong relationship between schools and parents is imperative for the success of an instructional technology program. Some common goals include parent access to available technology in schools, dial-up access for parents from home, electronic bulletin boards for parents to share ideas and information, and active training opportunities for parents to use computers.

Many district administrators, if not school boards themselves, regard parents as the ultimate consumers of public education services. Although we do not intend to downplay the importance of the student as client, parents play an undeniable role in the education of their children—or they should. The 46 million students are represented first and foremost by nearly 28 million parents (NCES, 2000). And, as school advocates, parents can have either a positive or negative influence in the advancement of instructional technology.

Impact on the Technology Facade: question 9.   Parents are expected to concern themselves with nearly all the questions in the Checklist. However, question 9 most directly embraces the participation of parents by their presence on a formal technology committee.

COMMUNITY AND CORPORATE LEADERS

Community and business leaders are easily recognized by their position (formal leadership role), reputation (nominal leadership role), social participation, influence (informal leadership role), and decision-making impact.

The costs of technology are substantial and can be shouldered only if the public, private, and business sectors—along with all levels of government—work together. Effective community leaders are valuable to education when they inform the general public about the school's technology-based goals; establish confidence in the school's vision for the future; develop an awareness in the community of the importance of technology-based education for the citizens of tomorrow; unite parents, teachers, and the business population in meeting the educational needs of children; and remediate fiscal needs and budgetary concerns with respect to the purchase, operation, and maintenance of technologies.

Impact on the Technology Facade: question 9.   This question encourages the inclusion of community leaders (as well as parents) on any formal technology committee, particularly the Budget Preparation Team and Technology Planning Teams. They may also be valuable on the Hardware and Software Acquisition Team if the school is in the earlier phases of technology enhancement or must replace expensive technology resources (e.g., computer lab upgrades).

SCHOOL BOARD MEMBERS

There are approximately 97,000 school board members in the United States. They are responsible for educating 52 million students in almost 15,000 school districts, controlling budgets of nearly $300 billion annually. They employ more than 5 million teachers, administrators, and staff (Geer, 2001). Their "customers" include students and parents, teachers, school administrators, business leaders, local and state politicians, and, of course, taxpayers.

Local school boards have been entrusted with considerable legal authority; they serve as the executive and legislative body in the sphere of public education. Some of their responsibilities include establishing the objectives, goals, and vision of the district; determining the district's major operating policies and organizational structure; selecting the senior executives within the district (e.g., the superintendent); and assessing the performance of the district's employees, the outcomes of its instruction, and the success of its student–clients.

Impact on the Technology Facade: questions 3, 12, and 14. It could be argued that ultimate accountability for reducing the Technology Facade lies in the hands of the school board; therefore, several questions appear to be most directly under its purview. Question 3 charges the board with both interschool and intraschool availability of technology. Question 12 suggests that the board should lead the technology charge with a viable incentive system for teachers who embrace the future, and question 14 places the technology plan firmly in the hands of the district's fiduciary leaders.

DEPARTMENTS OF EDUCATION

State departments of education have collaborated with the federal government to strengthen leadership in educational technology. The U.S. Department of Education (DOE) established the Office of Educational Technology and recommended increased funding for the schools, including planning grants for technology, technology challenge grants, and networking demonstrations. The DOE has also heightened attention to federal technology issues with a range of programs, including Title I for disadvantaged children, the Goals 2000 legislation, the School-to-Work Opportunities Act, and federally funded research. Many states are following suit with their own brand of grant and aid programs offering the gamut of technology needs from basic hardware acquisitions, local-area networking, wide-area Internet access, teacher incentives, and student and teacher scholarships to advance instructional technology.

Since its inception in 1867, the DOE has spearheaded many of the innovations found in today's classroom. The use of Title I to level the playing field for schools without computers has been heralded as one of its most unqualified successes in the area of technology. The federal E-rate program has already awarded over $1.66 billion to serve the telecommunications, Internet, and internal connectivity requirements of schools.

State departments of education are also pushing the technology envelope with their programs. One example is the Link-to-Learn program offered to public and private schools in Pennsylvania. Link-to-Learn is the governor's multiyear, $166-million initiative to expand the use of technology in the classroom, including new and upgraded computers for schools and high-tech training for teachers. Link-to-Learn is also developing a community-based consortium called the Pennsylvania Education Network.

TECHNOLOGY COMMITTEES

The Technology Committee at the school or district level should represent every possible niche of the school community—teachers, administrators, staff, business leaders, civic leaders, homemakers, parents, and even students. Educational textbooks encourage administrators to "involve all stakeholders." Likewise, members of the Technology Committee must perceive their participation as important. Each member must be provided with sufficient resources to perform assigned tasks, and the committee chair must communicate clearly the purpose and goals for which they have convened.

The purpose of the Technology Committee is to enhance academic performance by using technology to facilitate instructional and noninstructional functions within the school; use technology for planning and administrative purposes; and develop and maintain a comprehensive plan to provide computer resources that are adequate to meet the academic needs of the school. The committee recommends policies and procedures governing the use of resources and actively promotes the acquisition or modification of equipment, space, and services.

Impact on the Technology Facade: questions 8 and 9.   These two questions underscore the composition of the Technology Committee. A viable committee requires two dimensions: scope of activity and depth of participation. Scope of activity suggests that the committee address the issues of hardware/software acquisition, budget preparation, curriculum design, and technology planning. Depth of participation awards points for representation from as wide a constituency as practical.

PRINCIPAL

The chief operating officer in the school plant is, of course, the principal. Recognized as the head of a corporate entity, the roles and responsibilities of the principal encompass instructional leadership, staff supervision, plant operations and maintenance, implementation of board goals, assessment (professional and personal), and vision and innovation. Instructional technology fits into several of these areas of responsibility.

The principal is the primary administrator of instructional technology— from technology planning and implementation, to upgrades and classroom application. Issues surrounding the principal and technology include primarily those of equity (equal access to students and teachers) and curriculum practice (successful learning outcomes using applied classroom technologies). It is not surprising to note that in a recently published survey of building-level administrators, the chief barriers to the effective use of technology center in teacher preparation. Yet only 15 percent of the administrators polled confessed to using technology themselves (Geer, 2001).

Impact on the Technology Facade: questions 1, 2, 7, and 19.   The building principal determines access to computer labs and classroom technology (question 1), both during and outside school hours (question 2), for teachers who wish to explore technology-based content material (question 19). Teacher preparation and in-service training is also the responsibility of the school principal (question 7). Finally, all methods of teacher incentive and classroom utilization, technology planning and implementation, and student learning outcomes ultimately rest with the principal.

Section II returns to the Technology Facade Checklist to discuss four very important questions. Questions 7, 8, 9, and 10 measure the involvement of people in a school's technology program. Teachers, parents, community leaders, students, and others who participate on formal committees make significant contributions toward eradicating the Technology Facade.

Section II—The Technology Facade Checklist Items 7, 8, 9, and 10

7. **What is the extent of technology training received by teachers? Select all that apply.**

	Points Available	Points Awarded
Initial training over 6 months old	0	
Initial training only within the last 6 months	1	
In-service training on technology at least twice a year	3	
At least two teachers per school are encouraged to enroll in formal instructional technology programs	3	
Training classes available on demand (scheduled with the technology coordinator, for example)	5	
Your Score (12 possible)	➡	

ITEM 7—TEACHER TRAINING

Purpose of the Question

The people of the Technology Facade are best represented by classroom teachers. They must be properly prepared for the task, and that requires training. Most schools begin their technology programs with teacher in-service training. Unfortunately, many also neglect to mature their teachers' skills with a comprehensive program of continuous training. Technology provides an excellent topic for follow-up in-service sessions throughout the school year. Technology coordinators are a source of on-demand training as teachers grow to appreciate the added benefits of classroom technology. Finally, schools encourage teacher participation in formal graduate programs, often linking advanced degrees to pay raises. Tuition remittance is an attractive incentive for teachers seeking their master's degree. Some schools insist on a contractual agreement that teachers remain in the school or district for some period of time following graduation in order to recoup some of the tuition investment. Item 7 awards 12 points to schools who are taking full advantage of all the options for preparing their teachers to become practicing instructional technologists.

Justification for Points Awarded

Initial training over 6 months old (0 points).   No points are awarded for initial training over 6 months old because it has lost any instructional value, motivational importance, or technical significance. Although the Checklist does not deduct points, it might be appropriate if more than 6 months have elapsed since initial training. Teachers, like students, need more than a hit and miss program of technology preparation.

Initial training only within the last 6 months (1 points).   Initial training receives 1 point if it has occurred during the last 6 months, and only if that 6-month period is within the current school year. Both conditions must be met; otherwise no points are awarded.

In-service training on technology (at least twice a year) (3 points).   Technology should be a recurring topic for in-service training sessions. Three points are awarded if technology training is provided at least twice during the school year. An example of a complete in-service training agenda is provided in Appendix 6.1.

At least two teachers per school are encouraged to enroll in formal instructional technology programs (3 points).   Schools receive an additional 3 points if they have at least two of their teachers enrolled in a graduate program in instructional technology. An example of a program of study is provided in Appendix 6.2.

Training classes available on demand (scheduled with technology coordinator, for example) (5 points).   Of added value is a teacher training program on demand—a proactive technology coordinator responding to the immediate demand for technical assistance in the form of promptly scheduled training sessions. Appendix 6.3 provides teachers with a prototype form for requesting training.

Issues to Consider When Assessing This Item

- Technology training is most effective when scheduled immediately before its use.

- Technology makes an excellent recurring topic for in-service training throughout the academic year. Week-long workshops during the summer provide teachers with concentrated sessions to perfect their technology skills and develop new classroom instructional materials.

- Technology training involves preparing teachers to use office productivity software, electronic mail, Internet research methods, educational software packages for the classroom, and the hardware and software in a newly installed computer lab. Training is very important for teachers if they are to remain current in basic technology skills.

- Technology education involves long-term preparation of teachers and includes subject matters such as computer operations and troubleshooting, hardware/software evaluation, technology standards, technology planning and budgeting, and computer-lab management.

- Training on demand is the responsibility of the technology coordinator, but teachers must identify the needed training, and administrators are responsible for scheduling times to offer the sessions.

- Tuition remission is desirable for teachers wishing to attend graduate programs in instructional technology.

- Technology in-service training is best held in a school's own computer lab, science lab, or other center where the technology is actually used.

- Teacher feedback is important immediately following a technology in-service training session or soon after graduation from a formal program.

- Administrators, technology coordinators, and technical staff enhance their own technology skills and appreciation for teachers when they participate in in-service programs involving technologies. The professional staff often come to better understand teachers' reluctance to depend on technology, while teachers gain an appreciation for the complexity of keeping all that technology up and running.

- Technology coordinators who complete a formal program in instructional technology learn about the educational implications of technology as a teaching tool and develop a background that greatly advances a school's technology program.

Recommendations for Increasing the Points Awarded

1. Implement new technologies (computers, software, audiovisual materials, etc.) immediately following in-service training so teachers use the demonstrated technology as soon as possible.

2. Ask teachers to propose technology-related topics for upcoming in-service training sessions. During summer workshops, provide stipends for teachers who attend the sessions and demonstrate their excitement for technology by developing new classroom instructional materials.

3. Identify mastery of specific technology tools as a year-long professional development goal for your teachers. Begin the year with short training sessions to permit teachers to practice their skills. Over the school year, present longer sessions with more strategic objectives for integrating technology into the curriculum.

4. Consider selecting two teachers per building to participate in a formal graduate program in instructional technology. Look for a program that has the following course objectives:

- *Technology and education.* An introduction that examines the pedagogy of teaching digitally and the use of technology as a teaching strategy. Networks, video, and distance-learning tools are common topics, along with school-related legislation impacting technology and the various leadership roles available in the field.
- *Instructional design.* A course that familiarizes the teacher with instructional design theories applicable to education is recommended. Instructional system design models provide a forum for developing text, visual, and web-based instructional materials.
- *Instructional applications of technology.* A course to prepare teachers to develop instructional lessons using available technology is critical. Distinctive lesson formats apply the many strengths of technology to successful student learning outcomes.
- *Management of instructional technology.* An instructional technologist undoubtedly participates in planning, marketing, and management of technology. A program in instructional technology should examine the multicultural differences and the impact of ethnic diversity of schools with respect to technology.
- *Instructional technology practicum.* The pivotal learning experience of the program, this course encourages teachers to return to the classrooms with a practical understanding of the applications of technology for teaching and learning.

5. Provide follow-up training on demand. Teachers should formally identify the needed training to administrators who should schedule the sessions as soon as possible.

6. Offer tuition remittance to teachers wishing to attend graduate programs in instructional technology. Most programs allow a working teacher to take two courses a semester (up to 6 credit hours) fully reimbursed. Identify programs that offer at least some of their courses via distance learning in the event teacher course loads or other commitments prevent on-campus attendance.

7. Avoid conducting in-service programs at distant locations, such as a university computer lab, unless absolutely necessary. Familiarity with a school's technology is important. But remember, when using your own facilities, the in-service training should not be interrupted by phone calls, supposed emergencies, and other disruptions.

8. Solicit teacher feedback as soon as possible following a technology in-service training session or graduation from a formal program. Feedback should not be voluntary because the school is paying the tuition.

9. Invite administrators, technology coordinators, and technical staff to participate in in-service programs. Foster open discussions on matters relating to the importance of technology in classroom instruction and the issues associated with managing a school's technology program.

10. Consider enrolling the technology coordinator in a formal program in instructional technology to learn about the instructional implications of technology as a teaching tool. The investment of time and money is worth the effort.

8. Do teachers participate on the Technology Committee and its subordinate teams? Identify all that apply.

	Points Available	Points Awarded
Teachers do not participate as full voting members	0	
Teachers participate as members of the Hardware/Software Acquisition Team	3	
Teachers participate as members of the Technology Budget Preparation Team	3	
Teachers participate as members of the Instructional Technology Curriculum Team	5	
Teachers participate as members of the Strategic Technology Planning Team	5	
Your Score (16 possible)	➡	

ITEM 8—TEACHERS AND THE TECHNOLOGY COMMITTEE

Purpose of the Question

Teachers should participate as full voting members of a school's technology committee. A total of 16 possible points are awarded for full participation.

The Hardware/Software Acquisition Team is responsible for new purchases of computers, network connections, and educational software. It also has accountability for periodic system upgrades to technology.

The Technology Budget Team prepares the annual requests for technology-related funding and monitors the spending rate for the current year's budget execution cycle. This team is also responsible for ensuring that a contingency fund is set aside to address unexpected equipment outages.

The Instructional Technology Curriculum Team focuses its attention on the integration of technology into the existing scope and sequence of instruction. This team might be organized to consider each of the primary content areas if enough volunteers are available to staff them.

Finally, the Strategic Technology Planning Team has oversight responsibility for the comprehensive design and execution of the school or district's technology plan. This question considers the degree of participation by teachers on each of the component teams of the Technology Committee.

Justification for Points Awarded

Teachers do not participate as full voting members (0 points).   No points are awarded to schools whose teachers are not full members of the Technology Committee. Some schools skirt the issue by assigning teachers as "advisors" or "mentors" in a nonvoting capacity. Others simply neglect teachers altogether when forming their advisory teams. Although the inclusion of teachers on the Technology Committee is the responsibility of school administrators, teachers must voice their objections if they are not included as participants in a process that so directly affects the instructional process. Schools lose a full 16 points to the Technology Facade when they fail to include teachers on one of the four integral technology teams.

Teachers participate as members of the Hardware/Software Acquisition Team (3 points).   Technology is a tool for teachers, and participation on the one team that will define, review, evaluate, and eventually select the hardware and software for classrooms and labs is crucial. Teachers would not be comfortable with parents, administrators, and community leaders selecting textbooks or audiovisual films. Yet many teachers relinquish their responsibility for the selection of computer hardware, laserdisc programs, and educational software materials. Participation on the Hardware/Software Acquisition Team encompasses more than computers. It ensures that professional educators have a voice in using all forms of classroom technology.

Teachers participate as members of the Technology Budget Preparation Team (3 points).   The Budget Team controls the financial resources committed to the growth of technology in the school. Outside interests from parents, administrators, and particularly community members must be offset by the vested interest of the classroom teacher. Budget preparation ensures that the limited funds available for securing, updating, and integrating technology are spent wisely.

Teachers participate as members of the Instructional Technology Curriculum Team (5 points).   A logical (and typically noncontroversial) aspect of teacher involvement is the Technology Curriculum Team. Teachers understand their curricular goals, and most noneducators defer to their judgment when it comes to integrating technology into academic disciplines. This team, however, is often forgotten during the formation of a technology committee; thus, the justification for the additional 5 points.

Teachers participate as members of the Strategic Technology Planning Team (5 points).   Technology planning relates to the overall operation and management of a comprehensive technology program. Policies and procedures, originating in this team's deliberative meetings, directly affect the use of technology for teaching. For example, issues regarding student access to the Internet and the related responsibilities of the teacher, parent, students, and staff are developed and disseminated from this team and deserve input from the classroom teacher. The Strategic Planning Team is second only to the Curriculum Team in importance with regard to eliminating the Technology Facade, so schools are awarded 5 points if teachers participate on this team.

Issues to Consider When Assessing This Item

- Next to students, the classroom teacher is often the most overlooked participant when it comes to membership on the school or district Technology Committee.
- Hardware and software is often acquired from questionable sources, at least as far as sound educational principles are concerned. These include grocery store promotions ("Save your food store receipts for a free computer"), local business give-aways ("Please accept our generous offer of these old, outdated machines that we cannot possibly use any longer"), and breakfast cereal coupons ("Just save eight gazillion box tops for one

copy of our free math software"). Planning a sound technology program is difficult at best with technology acquired in this manner.

■ Curriculum committees are most likely to involve teachers because of the obvious application to teaching. Besides, classroom issues are not usually the most interesting aspect of technology.

■ Planning technology cannot hope to be successful without teacher commitment to its actual implementation in the classroom. Teachers must be prepared technically, pedagogically, and socially to participate on the school's Technology Committee.

■ First-year teachers are likely to be the most technically astute members of the faculty, having recently graduated from schools of education that offer instructional technology. Seasoned teachers are likely to be the most content astute members of the faculty, having immersed themselves in subject matter research, presentation, and assessment for the longest time.

■ Participation by teachers on the technology committee and its various teams deserves compensation as evidence of the administrator's allegiance to instructional technology and the value placed on the teacher's time.

Recommendations for Increasing the Points Awarded

1. Make teachers the *first* members of a newly formed school or district technology committee. If committees already exist, ensure that teachers are represented.

2. Staff the Technology Committee with nine to eleven individuals; at least two or three members should be teachers. Staff each technology team with five to seven individuals; at least one or two members should be teachers.

3. Do not allow store promotions, local businesses, and coupons to dictate your technology program. Do not accept technology that teachers find unacceptable for classroom application.

4. Teachers must participate on technology budget teams to ensure they guide the expenditure of limited resources on new systems, upgrades to existing technology, and technical support.

5. Teachers must participate on technology curriculum teams because of their direct application to the classroom.

6. Teachers must participate on technology planning teams to foster a commitment to the real-world implementation of technology in the classroom.

7. Select your best teachers to represent the staff. Select teacher–innovators who are both technically and pedagogically minded to teach with technology.

8. Select first-year teachers who have recently graduated from schools of education that offer instructional technology in their teacher preparation programs to participate on the more technically demanding teams. Make instructional technology a criterion during preselection interviews for all new teachers.

9. Select seasoned teachers in subject matter research, presentation, and assessment to participate on the more content-demanding teams.

10. Offer teachers who participate on the Technology Committee some form of compensation such as compensatory time off, first opportunity to attend conferences and workshops, and release time.

9. **Do parents, community leaders, alumni, and students participate on the Technology Committee and its subordinate teams? Identify all that apply.**

	Points Available	Points Awarded
They do not participate as voting members	0	
They participate as members of the Hardware/ Software Acquisition Team	3	
They participate as members of the Technology Budget Preparation Team	3	
They participate as members of the Instructional Technology Curriculum Team	5	
They participate as members of the Strategic Technology Planning Team	5	
Your Score (16 possible)	➡	

ITEM 9—OTHER PARTICIPATION ON THE TECHNOLOGY COMMITTEE

Purpose of the Question

Planning, funding, operating, and managing a school technology plan is an awesome task demanding as much involvement as possible. Sixteen possible points are awarded for participation by parents, students, and the community. See the discussion of item 8 on page 92 for a description of the focus of each of the four component teams.

Justification for Points Awarded

They do not participate as full voting members (0 points).   No points are awarded to schools that fail to involve parents, community leaders, alumni, and students as full members of the Technology Committee, even if they must actively solicit volunteers. Several concerned parents attending periodic PTA meetings is not satisfactory to warrant points. Neither are a few business leaders participating in unscheduled visits to tour the computer lab. To receive points, these individuals must be integral members of a regularly scheduled committee meeting.

They participate as members of the Hardware/Software Acquisition Team (3 points).   Community members represent a wide array of professions and vocations that offer significant contributions to the advancement of technology in schools. Salespeople, financial experts, and procurement advisors may assist with technology decisions, such as whether to lease or purchase hardware and software. Computer professionals can help select the right technology. Communications experts can offer advice regarding installation of network hubs and Internet connectivity. Parents and alumni are skillful fundraisers, whereas students are able to quickly assess whether prospective equipment and programs are suitable to their particular brand of learning. Participation by these individuals adds educational value to the hardware and software obtained by the Acquisition Team.

They participate as members of the Technology Budget Preparation Team (3 points).   Accountants, tax auditors, and budget preparation specialists are well-suited for this team. Members must actively avoid any activity that might be perceived as a conflict of interest. One example would be dual membership on both the budget and acquisition teams. Students are not particularly appropriate for this team, so points are awarded if this team contains only community leaders and parents.

They participate as members of the Instructional Technology Curriculum Team (5 points).   A less likely team to staff with community leaders or parents would be the Technology Curriculum Team unless, of course, those individuals have an education-related background. Local elementary and secondary teachers are particularly appropriate for this team. Also high on the list of excellent candidates would be faculty of higher education institutions if they teach technology or in a field where technology is integral.

Finally, corporate trainers are especially well-versed in the most up-to-date aspects of instructional technology, where the "bottom line" of classroom training is found in increased sales and better customer service. Students should be represented on the Technology Curriculum Team to provide evaluative feedback on the strengths and weaknesses of the technologies under consideration. With some guidance by their teachers, they contribute extensively to appropriate classroom technology.

They participate as members of the Strategic Technology Planning Team (5 points).   Similar to the Budget Preparation Team, strategic planning calls for a level of maturity that most students do not possess; therefore, they are probably not suitable for this team. No points are lost because of their non-participation. However, many community leaders and parents have a vested interest in the advancement of technology in their local school system. Strategic planning differs from tactical planning in its scope; strategic planning typically covers a 3-to-5-year period, whereas tactical planning is typically limited to the current academic year. Some possible areas of strategic planning include the replacement of outdated computers in the lab, hiring a technology coordinator or computer technicians to support the program, and offering weekend computer skills classes for senior citizens. If the Strategic Technology Planning Team includes community members and parents in addition to teachers, as noted in question 8, the full 5 points should be awarded.

Issues to Consider When Assessing This Item

- Students are often overlooked as members of a school's Technology Committee. Parents are also frequently neglected, and administrators tend to avoid participation by parents and alumni on school or district committees in general.
- Community members and business leaders must be concerned about the appearance of conflict of interest, especially with regard to the Hardware/Software Acquisition and Budget Preparation Teams.
- Many parents and students do not have the necessary background and experience to serve on some of the technology teams, particularly the Budget Preparation and Instructional Technology Curriculum Teams.
- Planning technology cannot hope to be successful without teacher, parent, and student involvement.
- Students may be technically competent to sit on technology teams dealing with hardware and software acquisition. And because they are active participants in the academic process as consumers, they may be a valuable source for curriculum-related issues.

- Compensation for involvement on the Technology Committee and its component teams is possible for parents, community leaders, alumni, and students.
- The ideal size of the general Technology Committee is nine to eleven members. Individual teams should consist of five to seven individuals, with minimal overlap among teams to ensure widest participation and involvement.

Recommendations for Increasing the Points Awarded

1. Include students, parents, community leaders, and alumni on the school Technology Committee. Include at least one student and/or alumni member, at least two parents, and at least two community leaders.

2. Prepare a written policy concerning conflict of interest governing participation on the Technology Committee and its component teams. All members should sign a statement confirming the policy and an understanding that any semblance of impropriety in matters under the purview of the committee or its teams should be reported immediately. Particular attention and monitoring should be paid to the Hardware/Software Acquisition and Budget Preparation Teams.

3. Select parents and students to serve on various technology teams based on their individual background and experience. Consider placing these individuals on the Hardware/Software Acquisition Team and Instructional Technology Planning Team. Avoid parent and student participation on the Budget Preparation Team and Instructional Technology Curriculum Team.

4. Do not ignore the possible contributions of students. They can be effective participants in the process of integrating technology into the classroom.

5. Consider training interested parents, students, and community and alumni members in programs dealing specifically with technology to prepare them for committee duty.

6. Parents, community leaders, alumni, and students deserve some compensation or recognition for their involvement on a technology committee. Possible incentives include honorable mention in the school newspaper or newsletter, letters or certificates of appreciation signed by the school board president or district superintendent, plaques hung conspicuously in the computer lab, nameplates with a committee member's name affixed to computers, or, in the case of a particularly generous member, naming a computer lab or seminar room in his or her honor. None of these recommendations involves a monetary reward, yet each will serve to enhance the reputation of the technology program and the individuals who are devoting so much of their time and effort to reducing the effects of the Technology Facade.

10. **Does your school provide direct access to the following technology professionals? Identify all that apply.**

	Points Available	Points Awarded
None of these professionals are employed in our school	0	
Computer teacher (Part-time/Full-time)	3/7	
Technology coordinator (Full-time only)	5	
Computer technician (Part-time/Full-time)	1/3	
Network administrator (Full-time only)	3	
Your Score (18 possible)	➡	

ITEM 10—TECHNOLOGY PROFESSIONALS

Purpose of the Question

A viable technology program involves more than teachers, students, and administrators.

The technology coordinator is the single most important technology professional after the classroom teacher. Responsibilities for this position include managing computer lab activities, preventive maintenance, and scheduling; maintaining a current building inventory of hardware and software; participating on the school's Technology Committee; training teachers to use new types of technology and new software; and initiating a program to help integrate the use of technology in the curriculum.

The computer technician is responsible for technology setup and inventory, computer and network maintenance, disk management, and minor equipment repairs.

The network administrator is the primary contact for network problems and associated security issues. Additionally, the network configuration must be documented, and training must be provided to all network users.

Finally, the computer teacher has overall responsibility for ensuring mastery of basic student competencies such as keyboarding, office productivity software, Internet exploration, and educational software applications.

Justification for Points Awarded

None of these professionals are employed in our school (0 points). A school without technology professionals is likely to be firmly in the grasp of the Technology Facade. The absence of these specialists places an entire technology program in jeopardy.

Computer teacher (part-time/full-time) (3/7 points).   Most states do not certify their computer teachers in instructional technology. Several reasons are offered. Some states are simply behind the "power curve" with respect to instructional technology; for them, technology is still untried and unproven. For other states, the lack of national and state standards limits their ability to certify teachers; however, this excuse is rapidly evaporating as standards committees and professional organizations are stepping up to the challenge. For item 10, schools who hire part-time computer teachers are awarded 3 points, and a full-time staff member receives 7 points.

Technology coordinator (full-time only) (5 points).   A full-time technology coordinator is awarded points toward eradicating the Facade. Because the technology coordinator is assigned the pivotal role of contact person, resource manager, and training controller, this position is not given to an overworked teacher with other responsibilities. Five points only to those schools who have an accessible technology coordinator on site.

Computer technician (part-time/full-time) (1/3 points).   Some schools do not have the luxury in their budgets for a full-time computer technician. Even though schools recognize that they need such an individual, paying the going salary for this professional is expensive. Computer technicians are often worth their weight in gold as they unpack, connect, and test new computers, printers, and other peripherals; track invoice and inventory discrepancies to ensure proper accounting for these highly pilferable assets; and repair defective equipment or inoperable software. To receive points, the technician must be accessible to teachers in an emergency regardless of whether the employee is full time or part time.

Network administrator (full-time only) (3 points).   The primary responsibility of the network administrator is to facilitate information flow among the computer lab, administrative workstations, and outside world. As the school's network grows and its dependence on communications increases, the job of network management expands exponentially along with associated problems if there is only part-time supervision of the network. Three points here, but only for a full-time, accessible administrator.

Issues to Consider When Assessing This Item

- A technology professional on the payroll is not the same as having access to that individual when the situation dictates; no one knows that better than teachers.

- Schools presently have a choice of identifying an existing classroom teacher for the computer lab or hiring a computer technologist who is able to teach students the basic computer competencies required to graduate.
- Schools also have another choice of hiring technology professionals as either full-time or part-time employees.
- A full-time computer teacher is required when the school has adopted technology as a curriculum goal on par with mathematics, science, language arts, and social studies. Part-time computer teachers are used when technology is still considered an academic "special topic," perhaps more on par with music appreciation, art, and band (not to diminish the importance of these subjects).
- A full-time technology coordinator is required to eliminate the Technology Facade. Part-time technology coordinators are often shared among several schools, making access to these individuals for classroom support virtually impossible.
- A full-time computer technician is required when the school has an effective technology program under way. Part-time technicians are sufficient for schools just beginning their technology programs.
- A full-time network administrator is required when schools depend on access to the Internet throughout the academic day. Part-time administrators are sufficient when curriculum is not tied to off-campus connectivity.
- Computer technicians are responsible for the day-to-day operation of all technology facilities, not just the computer labs. Their duties include prioritization of equipment repairs, installation of new hardware and software, upgrade of software, hard disk management, physical security, and supplies management.
- Network administrators are responsible for the operation of all communications resources, including computer labs and classroom computers, Internet access, network security, and often telephones, intercom services, and voice mail. Network administration is a highly technical position demanding years of experience.
- Technology coordinators are responsible for interfacing technology with the academic mission of the school. Coordinators provide in-service training for teachers and staff, manage all technologies used in classroom instruction, offer personal support to teachers interested in developing technology-based instructional materials, and coordinate the use of technology for administrative purposes such as public relations, sports, and parental communication.

Recommendations for Increasing the Points Awarded

1. Determine whether your technology professionals are accessible to teachers. Teachers are the best source of feedback regarding the convenience, availability, and utility of these individuals.

2. Consider the following sequence when hiring a professional s puter teachers are the most critical members of a viable technology without them, there is no program. Following closely behind the computer teacher is the technology coordinator, who often serves many roles at least until additional personnel can be hired. The computer technician is next as the program continues to add more and more items to the inventory of technology that must be managed and maintained. The network administrator is the final professional for schools with an increasing dependence on the Internet, although for some schools, administrators may wish to hire this individual before the technician is hired.

3. For states that do not certify their computer teachers, pursue a classroom math or science teacher excited about technology and willing to share that excitement with students. Hire a full-time computer teacher who understands the school's commitment to technology as a primary curricular area.

4. Only when a certified teacher is unavailable should you consider hiring a computer technologist as the computer teacher. Daily supervision by your best cooperating teacher is essential to ensure a successful technology program.

5. Hire a full-time technology coordinator to support the computer teacher. This professional should report to one supervisor, probably the principal. Use part-time technology coordinators only during the limited start-up period for a new technology program.

6. Hire at least one full-time computer technician for every two school buildings. Do not permit this individual's time to be promised to more than two physical locations. The computer technician(s) should report directly to the technology coordinator, if one exists. Otherwise, they should report to the principal to avoid problems with prioritization of workload.

7. Hire a full-time network administrator if the school's computer lab is connected to the Internet.

8. Make computer technicians responsible for the day-to-day operation of all technology facilities, not just the computer labs. Schedule at least weekly meetings to discuss, at a minimum, the status of equipment repairs, any planned installation or upgrade of hardware and software, issues relating to physical security, and forecasts of technology supplies.

9. Agree to share technology coordinators and computer technicians only for the first year of a new technology program.

10. Assign network administrators responsibility for the operation of all communications resources, including computer labs and classroom computers. Stay abreast of their recommendations concerning Internet access and network security. Expect to pay well for an experienced network administrator, and do not settle for a novice in the field.

11. Hire a technology coordinator who understands how technology impacts the academic mission of a school. The coordinator should be experienced in providing in-service training for teachers and staff and willing to devote considerable time and energy to assisting teachers as they develop their own technology-based instructional materials.

BIBLIOGRAPHY

Edvancenet, Inc. "Leader's Guide to Education." 1999. Retrieved November 13, 2000 from www.edvancenet.org/

Geer, Cynthia. "Preparing Technology Leaders: A Course Design for Teaching Technology to School Administrators," *AASA Professor,* 24(3), spring 2001.

National Center for Education Statistics. "Teachers' Tools for the 21st Century: A Report on Teachers' Use of Technology." 2000. Retrieved from http://nces.ed.gov/pubs2000/2000102A.pdf

Appendix 6.1
In-Service Training Agenda

I. The Pedagogy of Instructional Technology
  A. Background information
  B. Using the Macintosh operating system

II. Exploration of the Internet
  A. History and background information
  B. The Internet and education
  C. Using an Internet browser
  D. Educational web sites
  E. Personal Internet exploration time

III. Preparing a Lesson Using the Resources of the Internet
  A. Background
  B. Responsibilities for a successful lesson
  C. Preparing the instructional lesson
    Step One: Design the lesson goals
    Step Two: Conduct the research—a methodology
    Step Three: Form the lesson plan and instructional materials
    Step Four: Delivering the lesson
    Step Five: Evaluating student learning
  D. Conclusions

IV. Textual Instructional Lessons
- A. Use of templates
- B. Preview a document
- C. Create bullet
- D. Format your documents
- E. Use of fonts, styles, and types
- F. Changing tabs and margins
- G. Inserting graphics and pictures
- H. Proofreading tools—the spellchecker, thesaurus, and grammar checker

V. Visual Instructional Lessons
- A. Navigating PowerPoint
- B. Creating an outline
- C. Applying a PowerPoint template
- D. Using PowerPoint clip art
- E. Importing graphics
- F. Creating transitions and builds
- G. Producing transparencies, notes, and student handouts
- H. Distributing your presentation

VI. Web-based instructional lessons
- A. Web addresses
- B. Headings/fonts/font sizes
- C. Page/paragraphs
- D. Lists/numbers/bullets
- E. Images
- F. Tables
- G. Hyperlinks

Appendix 6.2

Program in Instructional Technology

Program of Study

Student's Name: _____

Home Phone: _____ Work Phone: _____

Email Address:_____@ _____ Semester of First Enrollment: _____

Current Teaching Certificate: Yes   No   Program: _____

I. Preparatory Courses

	Credits	Semester	Instructor	Grade
A. Introduction to Educational Technology	3	_____	_____	_____
B. Foundations of Teaching and Learning	3	_____	_____	_____
C. Critical Reflective Practices in Education	3	_____	_____	_____

II. Foundations of Instructional Technology

	Credits	Semester	Instructor	Grade
A. Technology and Education	3	_____	_____	_____
B. Instructional Design	3	_____	_____	_____
C. Instructional Technology Applications	3	_____	_____	_____
D. Management of Instructional Technology	3	_____	_____	_____
E. Teaching with Technology Across the Curriculum	3	_____	_____	_____
F. Assessing Instructional Technology	3	_____	_____	_____
G. Practicum	3	_____	_____	_____

III. Electives. Select additional courses from any of the following offerings to complement your personal program in Instructional Technology. Select any two courses.

	Credits	Semester	Instructor	Grade
A. Multimedia Design	3	_____	_____	_____
B. Multimedia Production	3	_____	_____	_____
C. World Wide Web Management	3	_____	_____	_____
D. World Wide Web Programming	3	_____	_____	_____
E. Digital Imaging for Multimedia	3	_____	_____	_____
F. Networking Operations	3	_____	_____	_____
G. Video Conferencing	3	_____	_____	_____
H. Technology Grants and Foundations	3	_____	_____	_____
I. Distance Learning Course Design	3	_____	_____	_____

Date Program Completed: _____ Date Certificate Awarded: _____

Advisor's Signature on Completion of Program/Degree: _____

Appendix 6.3

Teacher Request for Training

Your Name: _____ Grade Level: _____

Date Submitted: _____

Proposed Session Title: _____
Provide a short title of the instructional training you wish to undertake.

Training Description:

_____

_____

_____

_____

_____

_____

Provide a narrative description of the instructional training with as much detail as possible concerning the need for training, classroom application, desired dates for the session, and preferred instructor (if applicable).

Instructional Goals and Objectives:

1. _____

2. _____

3. _____

4. _____

5. _____

List the instructional goals and lesson objectives of the training. If you have additional goals or need more space, use the reverse side of the form.

Action Plan: _____

_____

_____

_____

_____

_____

_____

_____

_____

_____

To be completed by the proposed instructor and distributed to participating teachers during the introduction to the session.

■ ■ ■ ■ ■

CHAPTER 7

FUNDING THE TECHNOLOGY FACADE

Section I: Technology Facade Funding

The capital costs of technology are only the tip of the iceberg. For schools, the real cost to combat the Technology Facade comes in training, maintenance, and support. The life-cycle cost of owning personal computers approaches 10 to 20 times the initial price of the hardware (Blaver, 2000). Obsolete computer labs are replaced with more powerful computers, including sophisticated peripherals and Internet connections, and educational software is exchanged every 4 years on average to keep pace with the associated infrastructure. Each of these actions requires a more advanced level of understanding to effect sound fiscal management of a technology program.

EDUCATION CHART OF ACCOUNTS

Educational accounting systems detail a host of transactions that comprise a typical academic year. At the foundation of this system is the Chart of Accounts, a user-modifiable tool typically mandated by the state department of education and distributed to all districts and schools for implementation. Generally, it includes such major account types as instruction, support services, capital replacement, community services/relations, nonprogrammed expenses, donated services, assets, and revenues.

Most educational enterprises employ several charts of accounts to serve different purposes. For example, schools may create accounts for presenting a financial overview, expenditures, sources of revenue, major projects, or other purposes that a school board may deem necessary.

Technology, although inexorably linked to all aspects of a school's budget, is best served when considered as an independent fiscal entity and not merely as part of the generic general ledger account. Table 7.1 offers specific budget codes for each of several major areas to account for technology-based instruction, services, and expenses. Although it is not all-inclusive, Table 7.1

TABLE 7.1   Abridged School Chart of Accounts

CLASSIFICATION	ACCOUNT DESCRIPTION	BUDGET CODES	TECHNOLOGY IMPACT
Code 1000	**Instruction**	1000	
	Regular programs (elementary, middle school, etc.)	1010	
	Special programs (gifted and talented, reading, etc.)	1020	
	Technology-based programs	1030	Yes
	Regular computer lab instruction	1031	Yes
	Teacher technology incentive program	1032	Yes
	In-service staff and administrator training	1033	Yes
	Parent adventure into computers	1034	Yes
	Adult and continuing education programs	1040	
Code 2000	**Support Services**	2000	
	Student support services	2010	
	Instructional staff support services	2020	Yes
	In-service teacher technology training	2021	Yes
	General administration support services	2030	
	School administration support services	2040	Yes
	Instructional technology operations and maintenance	2041	Yes
	Business support services	2050	
	Central activities support services	2060	Yes
	Data processing (paper, diskettes, etc.)	2061	Yes
	Technology-related lease expenses (lab computers)	2062	Yes
Code 3000	**Capital Replacement**	3000	
	Furniture and fixtures, equipment, vehicles, buildings	3010	
	Computers/instructional technology	3020	Yes
	Classroom computers	3021	Yes
	Lab computers	3022	Yes
	Lab and classroom software	3023	Yes

TABLE 7.1 Continued

CLASSIFICATION	ACCOUNT DESCRIPTION	BUDGET CODES	TECHNOLOGY IMPACT
	Other instructional technology capital	3024	Yes
Code 4000	**Community Service/Relations**	4000	
	Child care programs	4010	
	Senior citizen programs	4020	
	Collaboration with community libraries	4030	
	Nonpublic school services	4040	
	Technology-based community programs	4050	Yes
	Senior citizen Internet classes	4051	Yes
	Internet access to local public libraries	4052	Yes
Code 5000	**Nonprogrammed Expenses**	5000	
	State, district, and intermediate unit expenses	5010	
	Technology-related nonprogrammed expenses	5020	Yes
	Dues to technology organizations	5021	Yes
	Technology conferences (travel, fees, etc.)	5022	Yes
Code 6000	**Donated Services**	6000	
	Parent Teacher Association	6010	
	Technology Committee	6020	Yes
Code 7000	**Capital Assets**	7000	
	Science lab assets	7010	
	Technology resources	7020	Yes
	Computer lab systems	7021	Yes
	Classroom computers	7022	Yes
	Other technology assets	7023	Yes
Code 8000	**Revenues**	8000	
	Sports programs	8010	
	Technology programs	8020	Yes
	Computer lab rental to community college	8021	Yes
	Internet charges to subordinate units	8022	Yes
	Senior citizen computer class fees	8023	Yes
	Charges to activities, clubs, etc.	8024	Yes

Chart has been modified to highlight technology-related codes.

does provide specific examples of how schools track this important instructional program. Whenever an account impacts the technology program, a "Yes" appears in the rightmost column. Only those programs are discussed further in this chapter.

Instruction (Code 1000)

Instructional programs comprise a significant portion of a school's budget since they contain funding for everything associated with the primary task of the school, from salary lines for teachers and teacher aides, to textbooks, education projects, and staff compensation programs.

Technology-based programs (code 1030).   Technology-based instructional accounts include the following:

- *Regular computer lab instruction.* All costs associated with the operation of the school's computer lab(s) go against a specific line item. Salaries and benefits for the computer teacher, technology coordinator, and any computer/network technician are tracked in this account.
- *In-service staff and administrator training.* All costs associated with the training of teachers and staff relative to technology are accounted for in this line item.
- *Teacher technology incentive program.* Schools offer remuneration, scholarships, in-house grants, tuition remittance, and monetary rewards for these efforts. Tracking these budgeted amounts does several things. First, it alerts teachers that such compensation is available. Second, it applies quotas for the two areas of stipends and tuition remittance. Third, administrators are better able to trace the results of such a program by comparing tangible benefits versus costs.
- *Parent adventure into computers.* This example budget line tracks extracurricular education programs. Schools that offer opportunities for community members to benefit from the technology provided by their taxes understand the benefits to be derived from a sound community relations program.

Support Services (Code 2000)

The second major segment of a school's budget deals with support service expenditures. Most schools maintain a separate line item for operations and maintenance associated with the business of education.

Instructional staff support services (code 2020).   The most common targets for general ledger accounts include students, instructional staff, administration, business office, and centralized activities, including the following:

- *In-service teacher technology training.* Separate accounting for technology-related teacher training reduces the risk that monies originally set aside for teacher training wind up paying for large outlays of more highly visible hardware and software. It also allows administrators to gauge the comprehensiveness of technology training across academic years.

School administration support services (code 2040).

- *Instructional technology operations and maintenance (O&M).* The daily operation and maintenance of dozens of computers, miles of networked cable, and a roomful of sophisticated communications hardware takes considerable skill in planning and budgeting. A lab full of computers sporting "Awaiting Repair" signs is a sure indication of the Technology Facade.

Central activities support services (code 2060).

- *Data processing.* Smart accounting frowns on a single budget line for all computer-related costs. Similarly, funds for instructional technology should not be commingled with administrative computer costs. Although most schools begin their journey into technology with a single cost center for all technology, chances are that the administrative costs quickly outstrip the educational costs. However, there will be instances when a centralized activity code is more appropriate. For example, the purchase of computer diskettes, special paper, printer ink cartridges, and the like are best purchased in aggregate.
- *Technology-related lease expenses.* Administrative versus instructional lease expenses are nearly always accounted for separately. The criteria for lease-versus-buy decisions vary, but without separate accounting codes, analysis of the factors associated with lease decisions are impossible.

Capital Replacement (Code 3000)

Technology changes daily. Schools must plan for the upgrade and eventual replacement of their computers, computer lab, networking components, and educational software. *Education Week* recently found that "some schools are upgrading their computers, but many are making do with older machines. Forty-nine percent of instructional computers in the United States are Power Macs or PCs with Pentium processors. But 19 percent, or nearly one in five, are Apple II's or PCs with 386 processors or earlier models" (Orlofsky and Herald, 1999, p. 1).

Computers/instructional technology (code 3020). The following technology accounts address capital replacement.

- *Classroom computers.* Classroom computers are often hand-me-downs from computer lab upgrades, and replacing classroom computers is usually the last project at the bottom of the year-end wish list. A 4-year replacement program is standard in industry, and separate accounts allow better management of these machines.
- *Lab computers.* Replacing classroom computers calls for a 25 percent annual capital investment. Upgrading an entire lab demands an even greater outlay of capital funds. Again, separate ledger accounts ensure that the computer lab is not neglected in favor of furniture, classroom equipment, or vehicles, which are more visible to the school administration.
- *Lab and classroom software.* Often overlooked, software must also be periodically updated to ensure compatibility with the latest hardware and changing school curriculum. Without an individual budget line item, software is neglected in favor of more tangible assets such as computers.
- *Other instructional technology capital* serves to replace such items as networking components, classroom equipment, and system upgrades.

Community Service/Relations (Code 4000)

As schools and communities ready themselves to meet the challenges of the twenty-first century, the stakes are higher than ever.

Technology-based community programs (code 4050). The community service/relations account proposes two technology-based programs that have been successfully implemented in schools across the country.

- *Senior citizen Internet classes.* Schools offering senior members of the community access to technology find the association of mutual benefit to all parties. Senior citizens teach technology to others as they learn desktop publishing, exchange electronic mail, and serve their local communities. They pursue lifelong learning with a willingness to share their knowledge with others. A budgeted line item to track the revenues and expenditures of such programs is highly recommended.
- *Internet access to local public libraries.* Many schools, particularly in less affluent communities, are working to provide libraries with technology-based services such as CD-ROMs, computer lab space, and access to the Internet. In turn, these facilities also serve the needs of the school for student computer access after hours.

Nonprogrammed Expenses (Code 5000)

Administrators cannot predict every category of expense that might be encountered. Nonprogrammed expenses are not unplanned expenses. They represent *planned* expenditures for activities and projects that do not fall within a particular category.

Technology-related nonprogrammed expenses (code 5020).   State, district, and local expenses are often placed in this code. Technology offers two specific accounts for consideration.

- *Dues to technology organizations.* Many communities sponsor technology councils, and schools find that membership in these associations fosters harmony with professionals and improves the school's reputation within the community.
- *Technology conferences.* For schools that are unable to provide other incentive programs to faculty and staff, conferences and travel expenses serve as suitable substitutes. Because these conferences are not part of the programmed expenses of the school, a separate account is established to fund and track such expenses.

Donated Services (Code 6000)

"Donated goods and services should be included as donation income to the school and shown in the statement of financial performance" (State of Pennsylvania, 1999). Donations are recorded at their fair market value, the amount the school would be required to pay if it purchased the goods or services. Activities of the parent–teacher organization are often cited as an example of donated services, as is the work of the school's Technology Committee and its teams.

Technology Committee (code 6020).   Technology Committee volunteers often provide valuable services in support of school technology. A typical committee roster might contain the names of parents, alumni, and business leaders with the skills necessary to wire a building with electrical and Internet connections, install hardware and software, manipulate a technology budget, or modify curricular materials. Track these contributions in a donated services account.

Capital Assets (Code 7000)

A corollary to capital replacement is the capital assets account.

Technology resources (code 7020).   Planning teams aim to replace technology based on the value of this account, then budget that amount as follows:

- *Computer lab systems.* An account to track the assets located in the computer lab provides the checks and balances to ensure that high-theft items such as laptop computers, printers, zip drives, hard drives, software, and diskettes are properly accounted for. Items of technology should be inventoried periodically; tagged by school administrators with model and serial number, date purchased, nomenclature, date last inventoried, and name of the account manager; and signed by the individual having fiduciary responsibility for its safekeeping. Inventories should be taken at least before school adjourns for the summer and again as students return in the fall.

- *Classroom computers.* A separate inventory of classroom computers ensures they are replaced as frequently as lab systems. The same information prescribed above for computer lab systems will suffice, and more frequent inventories, signed by the classroom teacher and principal, are recommended.
- *Other technology assets.* Schools may wish to identify aging equipment, technology by content area or department, technology by grade level, or technology by some other category (audio, visual, multimedia, etc.).

Revenues (Code 8000)

Often, a technology program is introduced into a school with the caveat that it must "pay its own way." Upgrades depend on generating revenues from evening classes and rental charges, for example. Code 8000 tracks technology-induced revenues so administrators correctly credit these income sources.

Technology programs (code 8020).   Many activities need technology resources but may not have sufficient funds for their own full-scale computer lab. Schools that rent these facilities for evening and weekend sessions find the income particularly beneficial for upgrades, enhancements, and newer facilities. Such funding is possible when the general ledger provides distinct line-item accounting. This account also provides funds to augment staff training and nonprogrammed expenses, assuming that statutes permit the internal transfer of funds.

- *Computer lab rental to community college.* Schools with state-of-the-art computer labs generate significant revenues by leasing their facilities to local institutions of higher learning. Even when considering before-and-after-school student lab time, most schools find it profitable to lease their labs for late afternoon and evening adult classes. By making computer labs accessible to the local community, schools also evidence good stewardship of public tax money and private tuition costs while fostering goodwill for many other programs.
- *Internet charges to subordinate units.* Districts and intermediate units will often contract for higher speed, lower cost Internet services on behalf of their constituent schools and buildings. Revenues generated from and payments disbursed for these services are tracked in this account.
- *Senior citizen computer class fees.* Retired members of the community are often hard to sell on the benefits of a school system they no longer use. Computer classes are an excellent way to keep senior citizens interested in the benefits of lifelong learning. Sometimes the seniors themselves

will teach the classes, thereby further reducing the cost of such a program. It is highly recommended that participants be charged at least a nominal fee for each session; the minimal charge ensures attendance, punctuality, and participation. All fees generated from this program should be managed in this account.

■ *Charges to activities, clubs, etc.* Similar to computer lab rentals and fees for targeted computer classes, other activities may benefit by access to a school's computer resources. Computer clubs need a place to meet; investment clubs need technology to research their stocks; and the scouts are always looking for sponsors of virtual field trips and merit badge programs. Any income, which should be minimal in this category, is accounted for in this code.

A true manager controls fiscal planning and execution. Of course, the chart of accounts proposed in Table 7.1 is provided for discussion purposes. Each district and state has its own requirements for fiscal accounting, and the title may vary. But to allow a school's technology program to depend on the whims of year-end fallout money, miscellaneous accounts, or general operating budget line items is to resign a program to the depths of the Facade.

Section II includes two questions specifically concerned with technology funding. Item 11 identifies the source of a school's technology budget, and item 12 addresses a school's program for recognizing teacher involvement in technology-based instruction.

Section II: Technology Facade Checklist Items 11 and 12

11. How is technology funded in your school? Select one.

	Points Available	Points Awarded
Technology is funded with year-end fallout money	1	
Technology is included in the operating budget under a miscellaneous account	3	
Technology is included in the general operating budget	5	
Technology is its own specific, recurring line item in the annual budget	7	
Your Score (7 possible)	➡	

ITEM 11—TECHNOLOGY FUNDING

Purpose of the Question

Most states employ a finance system centered at the district level because districts are legally responsible for raising money and determining how it is spent. State and the federal governments distribute funds directly to districts, and schools commit their teachers, books, transportation, and other costs from these amounts. However, a change in school financing is under way.

School-based financing may be just the ticket to ensure that technology-based programs continue to mature as a viable instructional strategy. Item 11 examines how money is controlled, and the four responses reflect the varied ways in which schools fund technology locally. A budgetary system that offers only "leftovers" from other academic and administrative programs raises barriers to a successful technology program.

Justification for Points Awarded

Technology is funded with year-end fallout money (1 point).   Government is well known for uninhibited procurement during the last month of a fiscal year. Schools, too, often refrain from purchasing classroom expendables and nonroutine maintenance repairs until the end of the year. Sometimes, technology benefits from such policies, but it is not a guarantee. Outfitting a computer lab with new hardware often defers to other higher-priority expenditures. One point is awarded for schools that fund their technology programs with year-end fallout money; not because the procedure is worthy of any merit, but because technology is at least recognized for its importance.

Technology is included in the operating budget under a miscellaneous account (3 points).   Meriting three points, a miscellaneous account usually budgets the fledgling technology program. As a result, it deserves a few more points than the previous response. Unfortunately, with this account, technology must fight for scraps among a field of otherwise nonprioritized challengers.

Technology is included in the general operating budget (5 points).   With this account, technology is placed in the same hopper as repairing the copier, replacing light bulbs, and charging the air-conditioning system before the beginning of hot weather. More often than not, there is very little money remaining in this account at the end of the year, unless it is scrupulously defended by the principal or full-time budget manager. This response receives 5 points because the general operating account is a step up from miscellaneous budgeting and far better than the year-end option.

Technology is its own specific, recurring line item in the annual budget (7 points).   Here's where we want to be. In this chapter, an entire chart of accounts was introduced for use when considering a technology program. There may be several individual budget line items set aside for this program. The full 7 points are granted only to schools who manage their technology budgets in the same manner as they control more traditional academic programs. Funding computers, software, network communications, educational software, and video-based programs should be readily identifiable in a school budget, and the topic of at least as much debate as new textbooks, increases in teacher and staff salaries, and resurfacing the parking lot.

Issues to Consider When Assessing This Item

- Exclusive use of year-end fallout money to purchase technology often results from improper planning and execution of the school budget.
- The miscellaneous account frequently disguises uncontrolled and unplanned expenses.
- A general operating account provides administrators with the discretionary funds to conduct the daily business of the school. Technology deserves better than to be managed solely from such a general account.
- A technology budget line places the program on par with other academic programs that impact student learning.
- Forecasting a technology budget requires the full technology committee to consider the recommendations of its budget preparation and strategic planning teams.
- Sizable technology funds are often necessary if the school is to take advantage of sales promotions, computer fairs, and educational discounts.
- Technology funds are often required to repair or replace malfunctioning technology. The older the equipment, the more likely this fund will be needed.
- Spare computer systems are encouraged so that teachers who depend on this equipment for their classroom presentation are not discouraged because of problems that are certain to occur.
- Technology-related expenses often occur early in the academic school year and in sizable chunks. For example, software site licenses might be renewable every year in September. Funds must be immediately available at the beginning of the school year to pay these charges.
- The chart of accounts provides the administrator a guide for budgeting a technology program.

Recommendations for Increasing the Points Awarded

1. The miscellaneous account should fund technology only if the program has a knowledgeable spokesperson and only until a more strategic budget can be established. For example, a miscellaneous account might be appropriate when a technology program begins mid-way during an academic year.

Temporary funding can be identified to support the effort until a more permanent annual budget is submitted and approved.

2. The general operating account should be used only to fund a first-year technology program. A competent proponent of the program should be responsible for tracking expenses and advocating for a more permanent budgetary solution.

3. Technology should have its own budget line and take its chances with other academic programs in the school curriculum.

4. The full technology committee should consider and approve a final proposed budget for technology after careful deliberation with its budget preparation and strategic planning teams and the school's administration.

5. Technology funds should be available to take immediate advantage of opportunities such as software sales promotions, hardware computer fairs, and educational discounts. Technology funds should also be available to repair or replace technology promptly, especially if that technology impacts the classroom.

6. Standby technology components should be strategically placed throughout the school to provide teachers with immediate replacements and spare support items (e.g., monitors, keyboards, projectors) without their having to seek assistance from technicians or administrators.

7. Consider the fiscal year when contracting for software licenses, equipment leases, and maintenance programs. Plan for large, technology-related expenses early in the academic school year, if possible. A good rule of thumb is to defer contract payments until after the first semester (late October, early November) of the school year.

8. Use a chart of accounts, such as the one provided in this chapter, to design a comprehensive budget for your technology program.

12. Has your school implemented a recognition program for teachers who develop technology-based instructional materials? Select one.

	Points Available	Points Awarded
There is no remuneration or recognition program to recognize excellence in instructional technology	0	
Excellence in instructional technology is recognized in school newsletters, bulletins, and school board reports	1	

A formal awards program recognizes teachers who develop excellent instructional technology programs	5	
Teachers receive compensatory time, monetary compensation, or other specific remuneration for developing technology-based programs	7	
Your Score (7 possible)	➡	

ITEM 12—RECOGNITION PROGRAM

Purpose of the Question

Developing technology-based instructional materials is a demanding undertaking. Researching the Internet, evaluating educational software, and sequencing material takes considerable time. Where is the incentive? Why should a teacher dedicate hours to develop a new tool for teaching? Schools must provide a rewarding program that will recognize and compensate the innovative teacher. Full compensation is not necessary. Tuition reimbursements or stipends are exceptional rewards. However, simple recognition in a school newspaper or formal awards program also represents appropriate reinforcement. Regardless, this checklist question attempts to recognize the importance of a teacher's time and effort as well as the benefits of integrating technology into the curriculum.

Justification for Points Awarded

There is no remuneration or recognition program to recognize excellence in instructional technology (0 points).   Without a recognition program, teachers view technology as simply another drain on their already overburdened schedule. Schools who performed poorly on the Checklist almost never (actually, in only one case in 75) recognize excellence in the application of classroom technology.

Excellence in instructional technology is recognized in school newsletters, bulletins, and school board reports (1 point).   This response provides an inexpensive, but temporary, means of recognizing innovative efforts. Only one point is awarded for this response, and only if the technology program is within the *first 2 years* of its inception. After a 2-year honeymoon period, the program should advance beyond newsletters and bulletin boards as the chief means of acknowledging excellence.

A formal awards program recognizes teachers who develop excellent instructional technology programs (5 points).   Awards programs are visible commitments to excellence. A hardwood plaque engraved with the accomplishments of a teacher toward the effective application of technology does more to battle the Facade than all the newsletters, bulletins, and school board reports combined. However, a technology awards program quickly becomes a disincentive for teachers if it is viewed as substitute for more tangible reinforcements. In other words, plaques should not substitute for cold, hard cash, and the nominees and winners must be deemed worthy in the eyes of their colleagues. Five points are awarded for this response only if the program has been formalized—that means a nominations and rules committee, a selection committee, and a recognition program worthy of the honors.

Teachers receive compensatory time, monetary compensation, or other specific remuneration for developing technology-based programs (7 points). Payment of salary adjustments, bonuses, and professional development expenses is the most appropriate form of compensation for teachers committed to instructional technology. A maximum of 7 points are awarded for this item.

Issues to Consider When Assessing This Item

- Preparing materials that incorporate technology often demands total revision of a particular instructional unit.
- Most schools sponsor in-house publications that publicize noteworthy accomplishments of a technology program. Examples include winning student computer applications, Internet projects, and successful uses of classroom technology. In addition, a school's advertised technology needs frequently bring desired responses from would-be benefactors.
- An effective technology awards program demands definitive selection criteria, competitive nominations, knowledgeable awards committee members, and tangible accolades.
- Recognition programs require coordination with local teacher unions, independent school and district policy reviews, and outside sponsorship by agencies such as the parent–teacher association or the school's Technology Committee.
- Compensatory time is a cost-effective instrument for rewarding a teacher's efforts in developing innovative technology-based instructional materials.
- Monetary compensation for designing and implementing an effective technology program is appropriate for those seeking to remain current in technology.
- Other forms of remuneration for teacher innovations include school purchase of new technologies for participating teachers, such as laptop computers, personal educational and classroom management software, and free Internet home access.

Recommendations for Increasing the Points Awarded

1. Teachers should integrate technology into their curriculum during scheduled program revisions. In-service technology training is an appropriate vehicle for exploring technical possibilities for any curriculum under consideration.

2. Use school publications to showcase the technology program. School newspaper articles reinforce successful teacher applications, and monthly newsletters announce a school's most immediate technology needs. Finally, publications recognize specific benefactors of the program, including repeat donors, significant business contributions, and the like.

3. Ensure the technology awards program is accessible to all teachers, from kindergarten through elementary, middle, and secondary school. Encourage participation in the selection process, and solicit feedback from all faculty regarding the award winners and their perceived contributions to the program.

4. Use compensatory time to reimburse personal time devoted to developing technology lessons, but only until school administrators complete work on a more tangible reward program.

5. Payment of salary adjustments, bonuses, and professional development expenses is the most appropriate form of compensation for teachers. Make every effort to initiate a monetary compensation program as soon as the school's budget permits.

6. Suggest to teachers that non-monetary remunerations offer an opportunity to defray personal costs, purchase personal technologies for their home or classroom, or offset the escalating cost of professional conferences.

7. Purchase new technologies as rewards and incentives for innovative teachers. Laptop computers loaned on a semipermanent basis, coupons or gift certificates for educational and classroom management software, or upgrading a teacher's personal computer are excellent examples.

BIBLIOGRAPHY

Blaver, Christy. "Total Cost of Ownership: Making the Most of Your Technology Dollar." http://hprtec.org/handouts/tcea00/TCO, Texas Computer Education Association State Conference, Feb. 2000.

Orlofsky, Greg F., and Jerald, Craig D. "Raising the Bar on School Technology," *Education Week*, September 23, 1999.

State of Pennsylvania. *State of Pennsylvania Budget Code.* 1999. Retrieved November 13, 2000 from www.pacode.com

■ ■ ■ ■ ■

CHAPTER 8

RESOURCES OF THE TECHNOLOGY FACADE

Section I: Technology Facade Resources

The third element of the necessary infrastructure is resources–and not simply those only related to technology. The Technology Facade involves a wide range of resources that must be brought into play, from vision and mission statements to the wealth of the local community. There is no better vehicle for discussing these factors than from the vantage point of a successful Technology Plan.

THE TECHNOLOGY PLAN

Research conducted by the National Center for Technology Planning (NCTP) revealed that by mid 1996, fewer than 30 percent of America's schools possessed a current plan to integrate technology into the curriculum (Anderson, 1996). Thanks to this organization's excellent *Guidebook for Developing an Effective Instructional Technology Plan*, those numbers have dramatically increased in the last few years. NCTP's boilerplate format to effective planning offers every school the structure for successfully documenting their technology program.

The Technology Facade Checklist references many of the components included in NCTP's *Guidebook*. Three Checklist items specifically address the areas of planning and resources. Item 13 establishes the existence of a plan and considers the amount of attention paid to periodic updates and revisions. Item 14 examines the important other resource elements to have in a technology program, and whether the school considered the most critical elements impacting technology. Finally, item 15 rates the most visible aspect of technology—computers. One sure measure of the health of technology resources is the current state of classroom and computer lab systems.

MINIMUM COMPONENTS OF THE TECHNOLOGY PLAN

Table 8.1 summarizes the elements (highlighted in bold text) addressed in a comprehensive plan to reduce the effects of the Technology Facade and increase your composite score.

Tab A: General Program Goals

General school goals are often expressed as vision and mission statements. A vision statement shares a school's foresight for the future of education and provides an avenue for discussing how technology contributes to this goal. For example,

> "Our vision is to be a world-class school system. In keeping with the mission and goals of the City School, we are committed to graduating students who possess the skills needed to succeed in an increasingly complex information society."

Rigorous technology planning is consistent with the broader mission statement of the school to ensure it is relevant and consistent with the school's stated objectives. Here is one example:

> "The City School is committed to the use of all available resources to provide quality instructional programs through which all students will develop their greatest potential, demonstrate mutual respect, work cooperatively to achieve clearly stated goals, value the learning process and prepare—in a safe and orderly environment—for a productive role in a democratic society."

Tab B: Technology Committee

Tab B constitutes the formal representation of the resources made available by the school or district to conduct a successful technology program. A strong technology committee is composed of dedicated volunteers and professionals, including teachers, students, parents, community members, administrative personnel, technology professionals, and local business leaders. Outside consultants should be added and removed from the committee as technical requirements demand.

Tab C: Hardware

A hardware inventory presents a snapshot of the technology resources used by the school. It tracks the various platforms and peripherals, and its contents

TABLE 8.1   Technology Plan Major Components

COMPONENT	DEFINITION	CHECK HERE IF YOUR TECHNOLOGY PLAN INCLUDES THIS SECTION
Tab A General Program Goals	Ties the technology program to the school's **strategy** for serving its clients.	☐
Tab B Technology Committee	Distinguishes the **key players** involved in implementing the school's technology program.	☐
Tab C Hardware	Addresses **hardware** acquisition, installation, technical support, repair, upgrade, and replacement.	☐
Tab D Maintenance	Establishes preventive vs. on-demand **maintenance** and roles of technician vs. coordinator vs. instructional staff.	☐
Tab E Software	Considers **software** acquisition, installation, technical support, repair, upgrade, and replacement.	☐
Tab F Network	Considers **network** acquisition, installation, technical support, repair, upgrade, and replacement.	☐
Tab G Instructional Resources	Addresses **technology for teaching and learning,** including, but not limited to, curriculum and teacher preparation.	☐
Tab H Assessment	Views **student learning outcomes** on the one hand, and value-added consequences on the other.	☐
Tab I Community Relations	Attends to the goals of high-quality **technology-based learning environments.**	☐
Tab J Fiscal Planning and Budgeting	Focuses on the process of **funding for technology** including budgeting, accounting, purchasing procedures, and revenue generation, if applicable.	☐

COMPONENT	DEFINITION	CHECK HERE IF YOUR TECHNOLOGY PLAN INCLUDES THIS SECTION
Tab K Facility Planning	**Space, power, ergonomic, and security issues** are linked to standards, equity concerns, and environmental questions.	☐
Tab L Auxiliary Services	**Auxiliary resources** include Public Affairs, Human Resources, Telecommunications, Educational Services, Pupil Personnel Services, Risk Management, and Purchasing.	☐
Tab M Training Plans	**Training** agenda and itinerary for teachers, staff, and administrators.	☐
Tab N Related Facade Issues	Includes **legal concerns, copyright infringements,** and **special needs learners.**	☐

should be restricted to faculty, staff, and members of the Technology Committee. A typical hardware inventory tracks minimal data fields, such as manufacturer, system type, make and model, location, and purchase date.

Tab D: Maintenance

Hardware maintenance includes several key subcategories for consideration. A formal, contractual performance criterion should be stipulated for the mutual benefit of the staff (teachers, administrators, staff, and students) and the providers (technicians, network administrators, and technology coordinators). A prescribed standard of performance ensures that all parties are aware of expectations and limitations.

The need for on-site technology coordinators and technicians is still under debate. Cost for on-site technical personnel is nearly always in direct opposition to the demand for quick response time for repairs. Established maintenance policies avoid misunderstandings, unrealistic expectations, and many other problems when using classroom technology. Whether to have routine maintenance or on-call repairs is not an easy decision.

Schools, like other enterprises, operate on limited funds. Difficult decisions must be made regarding employment and hiring policies with respect to computer teachers, technology coordinators, and computer technicians. The proper mix of teachers and staff is a delicate blend that is necessary for an effective program.

Tab E: Software

A software inventory presents a snapshot of the educational and administrative programs used by faculty and staff. As with hardware, software, too, represents items tracked on various platforms, and inventories should be restricted to faculty, staff, and the Technology Committee. Software inventories typically do not include operating system or networking software, but do track version numbers and upgrade schedules. A typical software inventory tracks minimal data fields, such as grade level of the software, its title and description, version number, publisher, number of licensed copies in the school, location, operating system and system requirements, and purchase date.

Tab F: Network

Network resources include a wide range of hardware and software that read like a foreign language to many educators. Fiber optic cable, local area network, network cards, transceivers, proxy servers, ISDN lines, dedicated telephone lines and modems, and access to the Internet are just some of the applicable items. These resources must also be inventoried in order to maintain, locate, update, repair, upgrade, replace, and reallocate them. Network items are tracked more by location than by type or model and typically last only 1 to 3 years before becoming obsolete with the rapid advances of new technologies. A viable network inventory tracks location of the equipment, manufacturer, type and model, and purchase and anticipated replacement dates.

Tab G: Instructional Resources

Technology supports broad curricular goals, and its resources may be categorized as tools for curriculum, teaching, or assessment.

Instructional resources for the curriculum.   Technology facilitates individual and collaborative learning opportunities, promotes a wider range of academic learning objectives, stimulates student creativity by matching various learning styles with multiple intelligences, and promotes higher-order thinking skills and authentic problem solving.

Instructional resources for teaching.   Teacher incentive programs reward faculty who embrace technology and its integration into the curriculum. Teacher in-service programs offer continuous, ongoing, and on-demand instruction in the use of classroom technology. And teacher professional development programs foster formal teacher preparation in instructional technology. All three program types should be considered.

Instructional resources for assessment.   Evaluating student understanding and learning outcomes is important enough to warrant its own tab (See Tab H).

Tab H: Assessment

Assessing a technology program requires a variety of objective tools, including surveys, interviews, standards, and more. Surveys, usually in the form of questionnaires, seek information regarding progress toward the personal and professional development of the teacher and the competencies required of the learner before graduation. Interviews may be formal or informal, requiring scheduled visits to the classroom to witness teacher performance and student interaction. Standards from professional associations and reputable accrediting bodies often provide the underlying philosophy for technology-based programs. Other possible assessment instruments involve suggestion boxes, mandated state and district reports, and the Technology Facade Checklist.

Tab I: Community Relations

Community resources include services and agencies that may be tapped by educators. Some are directed at the family, others at health and personal services. Table 8.2 is a short list of some community assets to consider when planning a school's technology program.

Tab J: Fiscal Planning and Budgeting

A school's fiscal services allocate funds, collect budget and financial information, advise public school administrators, and ensure financial accountability. This includes the following services:

Auditing, accountability, and information services.   This office ensures financial accountability and provides budgeting, accounting, reporting, and fiscal management services. A viable Technology Plan cannot collect, process, and assess the necessary financial data regarding technology without this important administrative resource.

TABLE 8.2 **Community Relations Resources**

COMMUNITY RESOURCES	PRIMARY CONTRIBUTIONS TO AN EFFECTIVE TECHNOLOGY PROGRAM
Childcare	After-school training classes
Homework assistance	Special needs learners, technology assistance
Recreation	After school programs, technology-based activities
Family/parenting support	Remedial technology assistance, fundraising support, technology loaner programs
Adult and parent education	Parent training programs, senior citizen training programs, revenue/income sources, fundraising support
Business planning	Assistance in technology planning and execution
Job services	Job-finder services for technology teachers, coordinators, and technical staff
Special needs services	Assistance in planning and implementing technology programs and services for challenged students
Volunteer programs	After-school staffing of computer labs, tutoring sessions
Local government	Demographics, data collection for strategic technology planning
Higher education	Data analysis and reporting, teacher preparation programs, in-service training, academic standards, curriculum development
Business associations	Nominations for technology committee members, discount technology purchases; services related to the installation and maintenance of hardware, software, and networks
Local associations	Legal consultation regarding technology issues; access to philanthropic activities; donation sources

Systems and management assistance. This office typically assists with school-oversight responsibilities related to financial solvency, including programs such as technology that are often identified as at risk when they are first initiated. This office ensures that the necessary steps are taken to maintain program integrity.

Categorical programs. Many state, local, and public institutions award categorical technology grants amounting to thousands of dollars. This office identifies and recommends funding sources for technology programs while simultaneously ensuring prospective benefactors that funds are properly accounted for.

Systems analysis.   Analysts advise the school about laws, regulations, procedures, and policies. They coordinate requests for local funding and provide support for governmental budget submissions. Systems analysts are the appropriate professionals to assess a technology program. They spot inefficiencies and offer recommendations for improvements. In other words, they serve as independent evaluators of a Technology Plan and conduct periodic assessments of its results.

Tab K: Facility Planning

A school district is responsible for buildings, classrooms, and laboratories under their jurisdiction. They must be heated, lighted, ventilated, and maintained in a clean and sanitary condition. They must be repaired, furnished and insured. Schools must be constantly concerned with the safety, reliability, economy, and efficiency of their facilities. An efficient facilities program benefits the advancement of technology in several ways and includes issues of maintenance, operations, and capital improvements. Maintenance is necessary to realize the useful life of fixed assets such as computer labs, network closets, communications backbones, and classroom furnishings. Operations encompass those activities related to a building's normal functions. Lighting, access to electrical systems, and environmental considerations are key considerations when integrating technology into the classroom. Capital improvements involve changes to the current design conditions of the buildings, classrooms, and computer labs through acquisition, alteration, or modifications that add to the value of the facility.

Tab L: Auxiliary Services

Although it is certainly not an exhaustive list, the auxiliary components listed in Table 8.3 are possible resources for a school's technology program.

Tab M: Training Plans

Successful technology planning focuses on teacher, staff, and administrator training. Well-trained teacher–leaders make sound decisions on integrating technology into the curriculum, and they assist their colleagues in developing their technology-related skills. The most common goals for training include using new computer and telecommunications technologies to improve productivity; creating multimedia projects; using the Internet as a research and instructional tool; evaluating information, software, and other media for

TABLE 8.3 Auxiliary Services Resources

AUXILIARY SERVICES	PRIMARY CONTRIBUTIONS TO AN EFFECTIVE TECHNOLOGY PROGRAM
Public Affairs	Handles media and public relations for the school, including press releases, communication to board members, school fact books, etc. Highlights advancement toward established technology goals
Human Resources	Manages workplace policies and practices; noninstructional recruitment (including technologists); health, pension, and tuition benefits; employee and labor relations; staff training and development; and other personnel-related functions
Telecommunications	Provides a variety of data and network communications services in support of the school's instructional technology program
Educational Services	Offers an assortment of instructional services supporting school technology, such as audiovisual technology, technology-based instructional materials, computer training for staff and administrators, audio and video conferencing, and, in some cases, World Wide Web access and management
Pupil Personnel Services	Staff serve as consultants and become involved with students and families when a situation cannot be resolved at the school level. They also hire home teachers to work with students who are unable to attend school, often employing online technologies
Risk Management	Responsible for identifying, evaluating, and minimizing risks and preventing losses. For technology programs, this office can become an invaluable ally to protect high-value technology assets
Purchasing Office	As a support service for the school, this office provides high-quality equipment, goods, and services for the lowest possible cost. Often overlooked, this department can significantly boost the purchasing power of a strapped technology budget

academic content; designing collaborative learning projects for academic content areas; using technology for professional development; and developing staff expertise in the use of technology.

Tab N: Related Facade Issues

Although many issues impact the Technology Facade, three emerge as particularly thorny. Legal issues, copyright infringement, and special needs students are important aspects of technology. To overlook any one of these areas is to place the entire technology program in jeopardy.

A section of the technology plan should address any legal issues surrounding the use of teacher-made instructional materials. Although this discussion seems more pertinent to higher education and its concerns over ownership of course materials, the quandary is identical at other levels of education. By establishing at the outset who owns technology materials, hurt feelings (not to mention possible lawsuits) can be avoided.

Downloading images from the Internet raises the issue of copyright infringement and fair use laws. Again, upfront policies elaborated within the technology plan guide teachers as they begin to develop technology-based materials, rather than after the materials have become integral to a lesson objective. Appendix 8.1 provides a presentation concerning fair use and copyright issues. The presentation is also available online at http://www.duq.edu/~tomei/L2L.

Technology is a particularly appropriate strategy for teaching students with exceptional abilities. A viable technology plan should provide for all students, including those with disabilities and those considered gifted and talented.

CONCLUSION

Resources account for 32 of the 200 available points (16 percent) on the Technology Facade Checklist. More importantly, a workable technology plan often spells the difference between a successful technology program or a costly failure. Even the minimum set of resources suggested in this chapter are sufficient to keep a technology committee productively engaged for months. Yet, unless each of these components is included in a technology plan, the odds of overcoming the Technology Facade are slim.

Section II offers suggestions for measuring the health of a school's technology resources. Questions 13 and 14 specifically relate to the technology plan itself: first, the existence and health of the plan; and second, its comprehensiveness as a management tool. Question 15 tells the tale of spending for technology by gauging perhaps the most visible technology in most schools: computers. If other questions in the Checklist produce less than maximum points, often question 15 surfaces as the cause.

Section II: Technology Facade Checklist Items 13, 14, and 15

13. Is there a technology plan for the school? Select one.

	Points Available	Points Awarded
No technology plan exists in our school	0	
The school is working under a general district-wide plan, but a local building plan does not exist	1	
The school is working on an informal strategy for technology, but a formal plan has not been prepared	3	
Yes, but it is in serious need of revision or has not been revised in the previous 2 years	5	
Yes, and it is revised on a regularly scheduled basis at least annually	7	
Your Score (7 possible)	➡	

ITEM 13—TECHNOLOGY PLAN

Purpose of the Question

Perhaps no single document exemplifies a school's technology program and the commitment of its administrators, teachers, and staff more than the technology plan. Item 13 exposes the currency of the plan and how recently it has been reviewed and revised.

Justification for Points Awarded

No technology plan exists in our school (0 points).   No plan, no points.

The school is working under a general districtwide plan, but a local building plan does not exist (1 point).   Schools cannot be expected to get out from under the Facade without their own technology program. Award 1 point if the school is using a boilerplate plan and is still in the inaugural year of its technology program; otherwise, no points are given.

The school is working on an informal strategy for technology, but a formal plan has not been prepared (3 points).   Three points are allowed if the school is still within the first 3 years of its program. During this period, developing and approving a formal document should be a number one priority.

Yes, but it is in serious need of revision or has not been revised in the previous 2 years (5 points).   The only way to ensure that the plan remains current is to assign that responsibility to a team within the Technology Committee; the Strategic Technology Planning Team is the obvious choice.

Yes, and it is revised on a regularly scheduled basis at least annually (7 points).   Hopefully, most schools receive the full 7 points for this question. A regular review of the plan is critical to defeating the Technology Facade.

Issues to Consider When Assessing This Item

- Many districts provide an overarching guide for technology in their subordinate schools. Because the task of integrating technology can be an awesome undertaking, this process should be met with enthusiasm and eagerness.
- An informal technology plan usually means that no one has bothered to write down the integral steps required to be successful—and that can get a school into trouble very quickly.
- Many plans are enthusiastically developed and adopted at the outset of a program and then quickly lose their novelty. A strategic plan is no longer potent after 12 months and needs attention to ensure that old objectives are addressed and new ones are considered.

Recommendations for Increasing the Points Awarded

1. Adopt the district's plan for the first year of a program, keeping in mind that within 12 months, the school should be operating its own unique program.

2. Develop a technology plan that takes advantage of quantity discounts, shared resources, and collective technical consultants whenever possible.

3. Do not rely on an informal plan to conduct the business of technology. The Strategic Technology Planning Team should prepare the comprehensive draft plan and distribute the document for full committee review and formal approval.

4. Schedule annual reviews and revalidation of the technology plan. Make these formal reviews an annual agenda item for the committee.

14. **Does your school's Technology Plan contain the following? Identify all that apply.**

	Points Available	Points Awarded
No technology plan exists in our school	0	
Vision/mission statement	1	
Demographic review of teachers, students, and community	1	
Technology-related purchasing procedures	1	
Periodic and on-call maintenance for instructional technologies used for classroom teaching	1	
Security plan regarding physical threats, human threats, and Internet threats to technology	1	
Formation and operation of a viable technology committee with diverse membership	2	
Impact of technology integration on the curriculum	2	
The uses of technology for lifelong learning, special needs learners, and exceptional learners	2	
A comprehensive facility plan for installation and periodic upgrades	2	
A formal plan for continuous evaluation, both formal and informal	3	
Your Score (16 possible)	➡	

ITEM 14—TECHNOLOGY PLAN CONTENTS

Purpose of the Question

The checklist includes a question that evaluates the Technology Plan and awards up to 16 points out of a possible 200 total points (8 percent) for its comprehensiveness. For schools and districts seeking to improve their program, this question is the logical place to begin.

Justification for Points Awarded

No technology plan exists in our school (0 points).   No plan, no points.

Vision/mission statement (1 point).   Technology plans with upfront vision and mission statements not buried on the last pages of a lengthy document merit 1 point.

Demographic review of teachers, students, and community (1 point).   Location, socioeconomic status of district clients, and population age are important factors in the long-term success of a technology program. Score 1 point for an analysis of the demographic makeup of the service region.

Technology-related purchasing procedures (1 point).   Procurement and acquisition policies encourage equipment and software discounts. They also advocate hardware and software standards. Award the school 1 point if such policies are referenced in the plan.

Periodic and on-call maintenance for instructional technologies used for classroom teaching (1 point).   Maintenance is worth another point if the school has an accessible program for repairing its technology. One point is awarded regardless of whether periodic or as-required maintenance is in effect.

Security plan regarding physical threats, human threats, and Internet threats to technology (1 point).   To receive this point, a security plan must meet three criteria. First, it must be written and not merely an oral understanding. Second, it must be in the job description of one individual and not entrusted to everyone. And third, the plan must be tested at least semiannually and evaluated/revised at least once a year.

Formation and operation of a viable technology committee with diverse membership (2 points).   This response reflects the importance of forming a formal committee to battle the Facade. To receive both points, members must be formally assigned to the committee; the committee must prepare, publish, and distribute minutes; and committee meetings must consistently have a quorum of 70 percent or better of membership at its meetings.

Impact of technology integration on the curriculum (2 points).   Curriculum is changing almost as fast as technology. The curriculum team and the technology coordinator should assess curriculum content areas and the impact of technology at least once every 3 years. If these duties are assigned and curriculum conversions are under way, award 2 points.

The uses of technology for lifelong learning, special needs learners, and exceptional learners (2 points).   Technology is an emerging tool for special needs and exceptional learners. Both ends of the learning curve benefit from a comprehensive program of integrated technology. The plan should include integration of adaptive technologies. Score 2 points for discussions of visual impairments, physical impairments, visual/hearing/speech impairments, learning disabilities, and exceptional students.

A comprehensive facility plan for installation and periodic upgrades (2 points). A complete technology plan contains diagrams of new buildings, intended enhancements to existing resources, environmental issues in labs and classrooms, upgrades to power and network requirements, furniture improvements, and additional classroom media fixtures (e.g., LCD projectors, computer carousels, etc.). Points are liberally awarded for combinations of these items. Award the full 2 points for any plan that has a strategy for addressing environmental issues and a tab outlining intended enhancements.

A formal plan for continuous evaluation, both formal and informal (3 points). Independent evaluation is the only means of assessing progress toward eliminating the Facade. The Checklist provides 3 points if schools maintain a staff member or independent evaluator who analyzes technology at regular intervals throughout the school year. Fewer points (1 or 2, at your discretion) are awarded if the evaluation is informal; that is, assessment remains the responsibility of school administrators.

Issues to Consider When Assessing This Item

- Vision/mission statements describe the school's future in broad, positive terms. Where will the academic program be in 2 years, 5 years, 10 years? How will these changes impact the ways teachers instruct and students learn? The vision statement conveys a positive attitude toward the universal advancement of education, whereas the mission statement is more specific.
- Demographics provide a snapshot of the school and its adjacent community.
- Technology is impacted by procurement policies. Effective policies seek to provide significant discounts for quantity purchases and to foster standardization within the school.
- Repair and upkeep of instructional technology is critical to a successful program. A rigorous program of maintenance ensures the best use of limited resources and adds longevity to the equipment.
- Security involves the protection of technology from physical threats (theft, damage, and the environment), human threats (hackers, disgruntled employees, and simple human error), and technology threats (viruses, illegal access, and blatant misuse).

- A conscientious Technology Committee attracts a diversity of membership, including but not limited to teachers, students, community members, business leaders, technology professionals, competent librarians, and the faculty of local institutions of higher education.
- Technology must become part of every course revision, rewrite of classroom content materials, and evaluation of course assessment tools.
- Adaptive technologies serve as remedial media for slower learners, whereas gifted and talented students benefit from the use of multimedia tools for enrichment.
- Facility design is a natural extension of technology planning. Location of new buildings, rearrangement of existing resources, environmental issues such as direct versus indirect lighting, speed of communications connectivity, purchase versus cost of ergonomic furniture, and classroom presentation media should be individually addressed.
- Independent evaluators offer the most objective review of a program and provide the best recommendations for improvements.

Recommendations for Increasing the Points Awarded

1. Ensure that the school's vision and mission statements address timing, technical support, personnel commitment and teamwork, and program flexibility. Answer such questions as, "What must we do to make our vision come true? How will instruction be delivered? At what levels do we expect our students to achieve? Will the community be involved, and if so, how? How do teachers view their future graduates?"

2. Conduct a demographic survey to generate a proper understanding of the school and its client base. As a minimum, establish the socioeconomic status and related population statistics; then ask the technology committee to assess the strengths and weaknesses of the community and develop practical recommendations for overcoming these shortcomings.

3. Implement policies regarding acquisition and procurement of technology. Do not inflate the technology inventory with outdated hardware and software. Ensure that each item meets the minimal standards established for the program.

4. Prepare a meticulous repair regimen, and stick to it. Decide early in the program whether funds are sufficient for preventive maintenance, or whether the school is only able to afford on-call maintenance to repair items as they fail. Reconsider maintenance policies during each budget cycle, and move toward preventive maintenance as soon as possible.

5. Implement a security plan that assigns specific responsibilities for the protection of technology from physical, human, and technology threats. Ensure that all teachers, administrators, and staff read and comply with the plan, and that security checks are conducted periodically to assess overall effectiveness and identify areas needing attention.

6. Diversify the Technology Committee with membership from teachers, students, community members, business leaders, technology professionals, competent librarians, and the faculty of local institutions of higher education.

7. Ensure that scheduled course revisions seek to integrate technology as a major component.

8. Implement adaptive technologies for special needs learners. Use multimedia as an enrichment medium for gifted students.

9. Prepare a comprehensive 5-year facility plan, and specifically earmark improvements required to advance the program.

10. Hire an outside evaluator to conduct periodic reviews of the technology program, and direct any recommendations to the school's Technology Committee and administration.

15. **Rate the computers in your school computer lab and classrooms. Identify all that apply.**

	Points Available	Points Awarded
Most of the machines are less than 3 years old	1	
Most of the machines are CD-ROM–capable	1	
Most of the machines are connected to printers	1	
Most of the machines are connected to the Internet	2	
Your Score (5 possible)	➡	

ITEM 15—COMPUTER LAB AND CLASSROOMS

Purpose of the Question

With technology advancing on a daily basis, it seems fair to examine a school's inventory of computers, both in labs and classrooms. This checklist item measures the age of the hardware, whether they are CD-ROM–capable and connected to printers and the Internet.

Justification for Points Awarded

The first item of business with question 15 is to define *"Most of the machines."* For our purposes, count the number of machines in each of the categories in the question. Do not attempt to calculate an average; that will not tell us what we need to know.

Most of the machines are less than 3 years old (1 point).   Machines built before 1998 are not fast enough to run most of the latest educational software. Systems built after that year are most likely multimedia-ready. If the majority of the machines in the school are in this category, award 1 point.

Most of the machines are CD-ROM–capable (1 point).   CD-ROM players make access to the newest educational software packages easy and quick. One point is awarded for CD-ROM capability, regardless of its speed.

Most of the machines are connected to printers (1 point).   One point is given if the majority of machines in the school are connected to printers, regardless of whether they are networked to a single printer or coupled with stand-alone printers.

Most of the machines are connected to the Internet (2 points).   The Checklist should probably award more than 2 points for connectivity to the Internet, but for now, that is all you get. The argument for 2 points is that today's schools are assumed to be connected to the Internet. If this is not the case, the school is likely to be deep in the throes of the Technology Facade, and awarding a few extra points is not going to help.

Issues to Consider When Assessing This Item

- Expect announcements of new technologies (i.e., speed, size, and capacity) almost monthly.
- Sharing resources reduces costs and increases accountability for lab and classroom expendables such as paper and ink cartridges.
- Sharing printer resources requires networking—another indication that the school has advanced its technology beyond the norm.
- There are two primary means of connecting to the Internet. Low-speed telephone lines use modems to connect to a gateway. Access from home is typically accomplished in this manner. Higher-speed cable access, on the other hand, is now available through independent Internet service providers (ISPs) and, more recently, by cable-TV companies who are quickly jumping on the bandwagon with their own high-speed access through the same wires that deliver hundreds of cable television channels.
- Connectivity to the Internet involves more issues and concerns for schools than physical wiring. With the growing number of inappropriate sites readily accessible to children, schools are obligated to show a good-faith effort to deny access to such material.

Recommendations for Increasing the Points Awarded

1. Computers older than 3 years should be replaced as soon as funds are available.

2. Schools cannot afford annual hardware upgrades. However, they can avoid proliferating old, outdated hardware and software by limiting donations of equipment. Hint: One school accepts donations of any machines with the stipulation that they will refurbish and resell them on the local market, earmarking the revenues for more effective technologies.

3. Consider sharing printer resources to reduce costs and lab expendables such as paper and ink cartridges.

4. For initial connectivity to the Internet, a low-speed telephone line is acceptable. However, teachers and students quickly find this method of access unacceptable. Reserve modems for intermittent access only, and then for short periods of time. A good example of low-speed connections would be the school library's access to journals or card catalogs.

5. Consider high-speed cable access from an ISP or cable-TV company. Many companies offer schools free connectivity or drastically reduced monthly fees. Also, many districts offer Internet access, securing large discounts for servicing many partner schools.

6. Send home a permission form for each student requesting parental approval for use of the Internet. Insist that the forms are returned to the school office, and keep them on file. An example Permission Form to Access the Internet is provided in Appendix 8.2.

7. Purchase filtering software before allowing any students to connect to the Internet from school. Filtering software protects children from the worst of the Internet and provides peace of mind when using computers for instruction. These packages also prevent unauthorized access to files or certain areas of your computer, which can make your school network more secure. Three of the most popular filtering software packages are shown in Table 8.4.

TABLE 8.4   Internet Filtering Software

INTERNET ADDRESS	COMPANY NAME	TRIAL DOWNLOAD AVAILABLE
http://www.hedge.org	A+ Internet Filtering Software for Christians	2 weeks free
http://www.solidoak.com	CyberSitter	10 days free
http://www.securecomputing.com	Secure Computing	30 days free

BIBLIOGRAPHY

Anderson, Larry. *Guidebook for Developing an Effective Instructional Technology Plan*, Version 2.0. National Center for Technology Planning, Mississippi State University, spring 1996.
Anderson, Larry. *Technology Planning: Recipe for Success.* National Center for Technology Planning, Mississippi State University, 1994.

Appendix 8.1
Fair Use and Copyright Laws

Online Copyright Issues

Considerations for
Electronic Course Materials

The Intent . . .

"The primary objective of copyright is not to reward the labor of authors, but 'to promote the Progress of Science and useful Arts.' To this end, copyright assures authors the right to their original expression, but encourages others to build freely upon the ideas and information conveyed by a work. . . . This result is neither unfair nor unfortunate. It is the means by which copyright advances the progress of science and art."

—Justice Sandra Day O'Connor

The Basics . . .

What is copyright?

Copyright is a form of protection provided by the laws of the United States (title 17, U.S. Code) to the authors of "orginal works of authorship" including literary, dramatic, musical, artistic, and certain other intellectual works. This protection is available to both published and unpublished works.

Exclusive Rights

Copyright protects original works of authorship. The copyright holder has the exclusive rights to

- reproduce or copy
- produce derivative works based on the copyrighted work (right to modify)
- distribute copies of the work
- perform the work publicly
- display the work publicly

Additional Rights

The copyright holder has additional exclusive rights, such as the right to

—claim authorship of the work and to prevent the use of his or her name as the author of a work he or she did not create

—prevent the use of his or her name as the author of a distorted version of the work, and to prevent destruction of the work

What Is Copyrightable?

- literary works
  —novels, nonfiction prose, poetry, newspaper articles and newspapers, magazine articles and magazines, software manuals, training manuals, manuals, catalogs, brochures, ads (text), and compilations such as business directories

- musical works
  —songs, advertising, jingles, and instrumentals

- dramatic works
  —plays, operas, and skits

What is Copyrightable?

- pantomimes and choreographic works
  —ballets, modern dance, jazz dance, and mime works

- pictorial, graphic and sculptural works
  —photographs, posters, maps, paintings, drawings, graphic art, display ads, cartoon strips and cartoon characters, stuffed animals, statues, paintings, and works of fine art

What Is Copyrightable?

- motion pictures and other A/V works
  —movies, documentaries, travelogues, training films and video, television shows, television ads, and interactive multimedia works

- sound recordings
  —recordings of music, sounds, or words

- computer software

- personal electronic mail

What Is *Not* Copyrightable?

- ideas or concepts
  —only novel expression of ideas or concepts

- lists (showing no originality)
  —alphabetically sorted lists

- factual information
  —public records, court transcripts, statistics

- titles or short phrases

Features of Copyright Protection

- copyright protection begins at the time the work is created in fixed form
- the copyright immediately becomes assigned to the author who created the work
- only the author or those deriving their rights through the author can rightfully claim copyright
- in the case of works made for hire, the employer and not the employee is considered to be the author
- duration is life + 50 years for work created after 1/1/78

Protecting Your Electronic Works

- no publication or registration is required to secure copyright

- copyright is secured automatically when the work is created, and a work is "created" when it is fixed in a copy for the first time

- "copies" are material objects from which a work can be read or visually perceived either directly or with the aid of a machine or device, such as books, manuscripts, sheet music, film, videotape, or microfilm

Protecting Your Electronic Works

- the use of a copyright notice is no longer required under U.S. law, although it is often beneficial

- use of the notice informs the public that the work is protected by copyright, identifies the copyright owner, and shows the year of first publication

- departmental and administrative pages at Duquesne automatically display a copyright notice at the bottom of each web page

- personal web pages can include copyright information, if applicable

Including the Copyright Symbol

- the notice of copyright is usually displayed in the following format:

  © 1997 John Doe

- standard University copyright:

  Copyright © 1998 Duquesne University

How to Avoid Violating Copyright Law

1. create your own content and materials

2. stay within educational Fair Use guidelines

3. use royalty-free, or public domain materials

4. get the permission of the copyright holder

Creating Own Resources

If you use own writing, illustrations, photos, recordings, and data, you are reasonably certain not to be violating copyright laws.

There are a number of resources on campus that you can use to format your writings, scan photos, or record sound and video.

The Faculty Development Studio, ext. 4611, provides equipment and consulting to help create original resources.

Fair Use and Online Resources

Fair Use allows for the educational use of resources without obtaining permission from the copyright holder. Fair Use is governed by four criteria.

1. limited access to the resources

2. limited time of use

3. limited quantity or portion used

4. limited commercial effect to the author

Fair Use Considerations

Text:

    up to 10% or 1000 words of a work

    poem of less than 250 words

    no more than 3 poems by one poet

    no more than 5 poems from an anthology

Fair Use Considerations

Illustrations and Photographs:

    no more than 5 from any individual artist

    no more than 10% or 15 from collective works

    if you can link to the image from another web site, then do that

    if the image is available, at reasonable cost, for sale or licensing, then do that

Fair Use Considerations

Moving Images and Music:

    no more than 10% or 3 minutes from any video or animation

    no more than 10% or 30 seconds from any musical work

Permission and Online Resources

Permission from the copyright holder is needed if you wish to use resources in ways that would not be protected by Fair Use. These might be

1. selections larger than Fair Use allows
2. permanent or recurring uses
3. widely distributed uses
4. uses with potential commercial implications

Royalty-Free and Public Domain Resources

Resources that have passed into, or have been declared "in" the public domain may be used without permission. Royalty-free resources may be used according to the provisions of their license.

Public Domain
1. resources with expired copyrights
2. certain resources owned with public funds

Royalty-free
3. stock photo/music libraries and clip-art discs

Resources

- Copyright basics (your first stop. . . .)
  —http://lcweb.loc.gov/copyright/circs/circ1.html
- U.S. Copyright Office Home Page
  —http://lcweb.loc.gov/copyright/
- Copyright Clearance Center Online
  —http://www.copyright.com
- Multimedia guidelines
  —http://lcweb.loc.gov/copyright/circs/circ55

Appendix 8.2

Permission Form to Access the Internet

Permission to Access the Internet from School

To: Parents of John Q. Student

Please complete the parental endorsement that follows. Mail the form to the school office at the address shown below, or ensure that your child returns the form for you. Please print carefully. When the form is received, a confirmation will be sent from the office secretary.

Note to Parents: We make a sincere effort to restrict access to inappropriate Internet materials. A sophisticated software package filters out sites containing offensive words; they are simply not permitted to be displayed on our lab or classroom computers. Although this procedure is highly effective, it cannot filter unexpected or unintentional materials. We exclude inappropriate sites as soon as they are identified. If you have any concerns about Internet access, please call the school, and we would be most happy to schedule a time when you can visit our lab, try the filtering software for yourself, and explore the important advantages of using the Internet.

Note to Teachers: Do not send an individual slip if more than one child is from the same family unless the parent wishes to stipulate different access permissions for each child.

Student's First Name: _____ Student's Grade: _____

Parent or Guardian Name: _____ Contact Us Via . . .
Phone Number: _____ _____
Email address (if available): _____ _____
Postal Address: _____ _____
_____ _____

Teacher's Name: _____

Short Description of Classroom Internet Activities:

_____

_____

_____

Please complete the second page of this letter.

Please initial each description. Each item must be initialed before your child will be permitted to access the Internet from school.

_____ I approve of my child's access to the Internet during classroom activities as explained above.

_____ I understand that the school has made a good-faith effort by installing network filters to deny access to inappropriate materials, and that the teachers will closely monitor student use of technology throughout the class.

_____ I also understand that my child may be refused access to the Internet if he or she is found to violate the rules against accessing inappropriate materials as explained by the teacher or computer instructor.

_____ I do not hold the school responsible for unauthorized access to inappropriate materials by my child.

_____   _____
Child's signature   Date
(If the child is over 12 years old)

_____   _____
Parent's signature   Date

_____   _____
Teacher's signature   Date

Mail permission form to:
School Office
c/o Computer Teacher
999 Rockdale Avenue
Citywide PA, 15111

▪ ▪ ▪ ▪ ▪ ▬▬▬▬▬▬▬▬▬▬▬▬▬▬▬▬▬▬▬▬

PART IV

A VIABLE INSTRUCTIONAL STRATEGY

> *The Technology Facade: "The use of technology in a school or school district without benefit of the necessary infrastructure to adequately support its use as **a viable instructional strategy.**"*

Teaching children and adults has always demanded a rational, well-founded strategy; a characteristic that takes on even more importance when using instructional technology. Too often, teachers must adopt sophisticated lessons prepared by technologists who understand little about whether the materials address specific classroom objectives. Educators must recognize the effective application of technology as another viable instructional strategy along with its strengths and weaknesses, potential and imperfections, and vision for teaching. Technology provides new avenues for student exploration. Animation software, hypermedia, instructional software, simulations, and videodiscs offer innumerable possibilities for tailoring instruction to an individual student's needs. An adventurous spirit is a key prerequisite, along with some structure to guide those first tentative steps in preparing classroom lessons using technology.

Jerrold E. Kemp's book *Designing Effective Instruction* offers nine elements to guide the educator through the design of a lesson (2000). Steps 1 through 5 address the challenge to concentrate on the instructional problem, learner characteristics, overall subject content, lesson objectives, and sequence of the instruction. Step 6 focuses on the progressive stages for designing the strategies and materials required for the lesson, while Step 7 encourages the teacher to select the most appropriate technologies. Steps 8 and 9 offer suggestions for developing student evaluation instruments and selecting the resources, instructional materials, and delivery method most appropriate for students.

For the Technology Facade, a viable instructional strategy demands that teachers (1) plan the curriculum, (2) plan the integration of technology, and (3) plan for successful learning. Part Four of this book discusses each of these elements along with the respective Checklist items that measure their success and offer suggestions for improvement.

BIBLIOGRAPHY

Kemp, Jerrold E., Ross, Steven M., and Morrison, Gary R. *Designing Effective Instruction*, 3rd ed. New York: John Wiley & Sons, 2000.

■ ■ ■ ■ ■ ▬▬▬▬▬▬▬▬▬▬▬▬▬▬▬▬▬▬▬▬▬▬▬▬▬▬▬

CHAPTER 9

PLANNING THE CURRICULUM

Section I: Curriculum Planning

Instructional System Design (ISD) is one of the oldest and most widely accepted schemes for preparing technology-based instruction. In *Designing Effective Instruction*, Jerrold Kemp's focus on curriculum design is combined with a series of practical steps to aid teachers in producing technology-based lessons (2000). Kemp's area of concentration in each step is referred to as key characteristics: this text adds practical implications termed "Teacher's Tasks." Read the characteristics first, then examine the steps that a teacher can take in an actual classroom application.

STEP 1: DEFINE THE INSTRUCTIONAL PROBLEM

Key characteristics. In Kemp's first step, the instructional problem is established. Learning goals are specified in general terms and later refined in light of the existing instructional program (i.e., the school's curriculum) in subsequent steps.

Teacher's task. In this step, the teacher establishes the academic content areas and selects the specific topics for the lesson, ensuring that not too many themes are targeted.

STEP 2: DESCRIBE LEARNER CHARACTERISTICS

Key characteristics. In Step 2, teachers consider their students' prior knowledge and experiences with the proposed subject matter. Each student favors a particular learning style, and technologies are available that best address these individual needs in the classroom.

Teacher's task.   Prior to conducting the lesson, the teacher identifies the target learner and considers any prior knowledge obtained from either earlier lessons or previous classes.

STEP 3: IDENTIFY SUBJECT CONTENT

The goals of the lesson are further delineated in this step, and their task components are defined.

Key characteristics.   To identify the subject content, consider the following questions: What content material is necessary to construct the instructional unit? Included in this step is information about the lesson itself, the learners, and the context in which the learning will occur. Where is the content information located, and what kind of lead time is needed to secure its use during the lesson? Possible resources include the Internet, textbooks, maps, audiovisual materials, reference books, and so on. What content information will ensure a successful learning outcome? And which technologies can best present the instructional unit?

Teacher's task.   Specify the individual elements that students must master during this lesson. For many teachers, these criteria are provided in national and state standards for content areas and grade levels. Match these elements with specific content area material provided in local scope and sequence curricula. Table 9.1 demonstrates how technology elements are matched with content material pertaining to an example lesson about dinosaurs.

STEP 4: STATE THE INSTRUCTIONAL OBJECTIVES

A major stumbling block for novice designers is the formation of the final learning objectives that represent the "best fit" of technology to positive student outcomes.

Key characteristics.   Developing learning objectives takes years of practice and reflects the educator's fondness for behavioral, cognitive, or humanistic teaching. Teachers must come to understand their own metacognition before considering their students' learning strengths. Metacognition is thinking about thinking, knowing what we know, and understanding how we come to know it. Just as an executive's job is to manage an organization, an educator's job is to manage learning. Before successfully instructing others, teachers must first become aware of how they themselves learn.

TABLE 9.1 Identify Subject Content

LEARNING ELEMENT(S) FROM NATIONAL AND STATE STANDARDS	SUBJECT CONTENT MATERIAL FROM THE TEACHER'S CURRICULUM
Using a personal computer	Locate specific web sites Download Internet images Print saved images to the printer Create a personal web address directory
Navigating the Internet	Locate given web sites Use the navigation icons in Netscape Bookmark favorite sites
Describing the most common dinosaurs in North America	Differences between an omnivore and a carnivore Periods when dinosaurs lived Anatomy, size, behavior, problems contributing to extinction
Selecting a student's favorite dinosaur	Locate black-and-white printout Color, cut, and mount prints
Developing language arts skills	Prepare 3–5 minute presentation Develop audiovisual materials
Presenting information in class	Conduct and critique the presentation

Take this short exercise. Examine Table 9.2 and complete the statements by checking either "Agree" or "Disagree" for each assertion.

Interpret the results of Table 9.2 as follows: For the most part,

- Statements 1, 4, and 6 strongly support the behavioral psychologists.
- Statements 3 and 7 uphold the teachings of the cognitive psychologists.
- Statements 2, 5, and 8 represent the preferences of the humanistic psychologists.

If your responses fell into a pattern supporting a particular school of educational psychology, consider yourself an advocate for their teachings. But do not assume that all learning objectives must satisfy only these criteria. Although it is important to understand where your particular learning strengths lie, keep in mind that students vary widely across all three schools of learning. However, when confronted with the Technology Facade, it is recommended to go with your strengths. On average, students learn better when the teacher employs his or her strongest learning style and selects technologies that best support that strength.

TABLE 9.2   **Diagnose Your Own Personal School of Educational Psychology**

AGREE	DISAGREE	I BELIEVE THAT . . .
☐	☐	1. Learners need grades, gold stars, and other incentives as motivation to learn and to accomplish school requirements.
☐	☐	2. Learners can be trusted to find their own goals and should have some options or choices in what they learn at school.
☐	☐	3. Teachers need to determine what students are thinking about while solving math problems.
☐	☐	4. Students should be graded according to uniform standards of achievement that the teacher sets for the class.
☐	☐	5. Students should set their own individual standards and should evaluate their own work.
☐	☐	6. Curriculum should be organized along subject-matter lines that are carefully sequenced.
☐	☐	7. The teacher should help students to monitor and control their own learning behavior.
☐	☐	8. The school experience should help students to develop positive relations with their peers.

Teacher's task.   Prepare behavioral, cognitive, or humanistic learning objectives depicting specific criteria for successful learning outcomes. Then select an appropriate technology. The following paragraphs present example learning objectives written for each of the major schools of educational psychology. Pay particular attention to the three elements of each objective—actions, tools for learning, and assessment standards—and how they differ, and how they are alike among the three schools.

Behavioral objective: Using a personal computer and Web address list, students will navigate the Internet; locate two specific dinosaur Web sites; and locate, download, and print at least two images of your favorite dinosaurs.

- *Actions:* navigate, locate, download, and print
- *Tools for learning:* using a computer and Web address list
- *Assessment standards:* two specific sites; at least two images

Cognitive objective: Explore the subject at your own pace and in consonance with your own personal learning goals. The Workbook will guide you through the lesson objectives to ensure that you experience the full range of goals and performance objectives targeted by your teacher. You do not have to complete the questions in the order they are presented. But you should complete all of the questions.

- *Actions:* explore the subject at your own pace; experience the full range of goals and performance objectives
- *Tools for learning:* Workbook will guide you through the lesson objectives
- *Assessment standards:* complete all of the questions

Humanistic objective: Students will share a 3 to 5–minute presentation using posters showing their favorite dinosaur and discuss why the dinosaur is their favorite. They will also explain why this lesson was important to them.

- *Actions:* share a presentation; discuss why the dinosaur is their favorite; explain why this lesson was important
- *Tools for learning:* using posters showing their favorite dinosaur
- *Assessment standards:* 3 to 5 minutes

STEP 5: SEQUENCE THE CONTENT OF THE INSTRUCTION

In this step, Kemp takes into account the sequencing of the lesson. With the instructional problem defined, learner characteristics described, subject content in place, and lesson objectives formed, the teacher is ready to pace the instruction that results in student learning.

Key characteristics. List the content information to be covered, and locate the instructional materials to be used to present the lesson. Reexamine the specific learning goals from Step 3, and add more definitive elements, if necessary, to achieve these goals.

Teacher's task. Lay out the instructional progression of each component of the proposed lesson. Match each component with an appropriate technology that appeals to the individual student's learning style and the teaching strategy identified in previous steps.

Steps 1 through 5 concentrate on the instructional problem, learner characteristics, overall subject content, lesson objectives, and sequence of the instruction. Planning the curriculum is examined in question 16 of the Checklist and addresses the issues of scope and sequence and learning objectives. Question 17 awards points for teachers who knowingly integrate behavioral, cognitive, or humanistic learning objectives into their lesson. Do not worry about recognizing the respective formats; the Checklist describes each school of educational psychology.

Section II: Technology Facade Checklist Items 16 and 17

16. **Has your school developed a scope and sequence specifically addressing student technology competencies? Select one.**

	Points Available	Points Awarded
No scope and sequence is available	0	
A scope and sequence addressing technology is available only for graduating students (e.g., 8th graders and high school seniors)	3	
A scope and sequence addressing technology is available for selected grades (e.g., 1st, 4th, 8th, 10th, and 12th graders)	5	
A comprehensive scope and sequence addressing technology is available for all students, by grade and subject area	7	
Your Score (7 possible)	➡	

ITEM 16—SCOPE AND SEQUENCE

Purpose of the Question

Scope and sequence is a tool used by educators to provide explicit learning objectives (scope) delivered in a predetermined arrangement (sequence). If planned correctly, technology supports this instructional strategy by facilitating individual student learning.

Although most districts and school administrators insist that teachers use a predetermined scope and sequence, they seem much less demanding when it comes to teaching technology. Some schools have constructed their own scope and sequence and are willing to share these efforts. Appendix 9.1 provides an added bonus for readers interested in implementing a proven scope and sequence for computer technology instruction, from kindergarten through high school. Question 16 provides up to 7 points for schools that use a formal scope and sequence for their technology instruction.

Justification for Points Awarded

No scope and sequence is available (0 points).   No one is accusing computer teachers of wasting valuable instructional time because they are unable to produce a documented curriculum for their technology program. However, the argument follows that teachers cannot validate the mastery of student skills without a scope and sequence. No points for instruction in this category.

A scope and sequence addressing technology is available only for graduating students (3 points).   Developing a comprehensive scope and sequence begins with the skills and competencies of students who are ready to graduate. Three points are awarded to schools that, as a minimum, standardize the technology expectations of its senior class, whether that is fifth graders ready for middle school, ninth graders preparing for high school, or twelfth graders on their way to college.

A scope and sequence addressing technology is available for selected grades (5 points).   Five points are given to schools who combine grades N–K (preschool), 1–3 (early elementary), 4–8 (middle school), or 9–10 (high school underclass) and 11–12 (high school upperclass). Schools that implement the program shown in Appendix 9.1 qualify for the 5 points.

A comprehensive scope and sequence addressing technology is available for all students, by grade and subject area (7 points).   The full 7 points requires a detailed scope and sequence for each grade level and a mention of how technology impacts key content areas such as mathematics, science, social studies, and language arts.

Issues to Consider When Assessing This Item

- Scope and sequence is evidenced by learning objectives that appear in a teacher's lesson plans. Technical competencies include lesson objectives that enhance learning by
  - Providing timely, unlimited access to data and information
  - Enabling and stimulating students to express their creativity

- Facilitating individual learning and teaching to maximize student success
- Providing diverse modes of instruction
- Promoting higher-level thinking skills to solve authentic problems
- Promoting basic skills and content
- Providing efficient and cost effective use of time and resources for management, teaching, and learning
- Facilitating the development, organization, and presentation of ideas to achieve intended purposes
- Facilitating collaborative learning and teaching to maximize student success
- Promoting the integration of curriculum, disciplines, instruction, and modes of learning
- Promoting adult, parent, and community learning

- Standards addressing *teacher* technology competencies that all teachers should possess are available from the following state and national accreditation sources:
  - National Council for Accreditation of Teacher Education (NCATE) (www.iste.org/Standards)
  - International Society for Technology in Education (ISTE) (www.iste.org/)
  - Action for American Education in the 21st Century (www.ed.gov/updates/PresEDPlan/part1.html)
  - Education Commission of the States (www.ecs.org/ecs/ecsweb.nsf)
  - National Education Summit of the New Standards Project (www.achieve.org)
  - Council of Chief State School Officers (www.ccsso.org)
  - National Educational Technology Standards (NETS) Project (http://cnets.iste.org)

- Standards addressing *student* technology competencies (i.e., scope and sequence) are also available via the Internet. Some of the better sites include
  - Radford Complex Schools Technology Scope & Sequence for Grades K–6 (www.k12.hi.us/~aliamanu/curriculum.htm)
  - Basehor–Linwood Virtual Charter School for Grades K–12 (www.usd458.k12.ks.us/Curriculum/Computer)
  - Andover Public Schools for Grades K–8 and High School (www.andoverpublicschools.com)
  - Profiles for Technology-Literate Students: preK–2 (http://cnets.iste.org/k2pro.htm), grades 3–5 (http://cnets.iste.org/35pro.htm),

grades 6–8 (http://cnets.iste.org/68pro.htm), grades 9–12 (http://cnets.iste.org/912pro.htm)

- Technology standards infused into academic content areas are available from state standards committees. For example, the Pennsylvania Department of Education includes the following:
    - Academic Standards for Reading, Writing, Speaking, and Listening (www.pde.psu.edu/standard/reading.pdf)
    - Academic Standards for Mathematics (www.pde.psu.edu/standard/math.pdf)
    - Academic Standards for Economics (Proposed) (www.pde.psu.edu/standard/economics.pdf)
    - Academic Standards for Civics and Government (Proposed) (www.pde.psu.edu/standard/civics.pdf)
    - Academic Standards for Science and Technology (www.pde.psu.edu/standard/science.pdf)
    - Academic Standards for Environment and Ecology (www.pde.psu.edu/standard/ecology.pdf)

- Learning With Technology Profile is an online profile tool that compares current instructional practices with a set of indicators for engaged learning and high-performance technology. This tool is available from the North Central Regional Technology in Education Consortium. (www.ncrtec.org/capacity/profile/profwww.htm)

Recommendations for Increasing the Points Awarded

1. Create a scope and sequence for technology classes. Convert the elements into recognizable learning objectives, and include them in approved lesson plans. Create technology-rich objectives that enhance learning and promote basic technical competency in all students.

2. Make state and national teacher accreditation standards the topic of an in-service program at the beginning of the academic year to excite teachers about technology. Encourage teachers to enroll in basic and advanced technology classes at local colleges and universities.

3. Develop a scope and sequence for technology competencies at your school. Use the web-based references in the preceding Issues to Consider section to determine the most appropriate skills for students.

4. Familiarize teachers with the proposed technology standards from state and national agencies. Make them responsible for infusing technology into their lesson plans, and expect them to demonstrate a reasonable level of mastery. Provide the opportunity for teachers to sign up for college-level courses in instructional technology.

17. Teachers' lesson plans should include specific learning objectives when using technology-based resources. Is there evidence of learning objectives that are consistent with accepted educational psychology? Select one.

	Points Available	Points Awarded
Learning objectives are not identifiable in classroom lesson plans	0	
Learning objectives are used for technology-related lessons, but it is difficult to identify the criteria for successful student learning	1	
Behavioral objectives are used. They include components of behavior (actions to be performed), condition (instructional tools), and criteria (assessment standards)	7	
Cognitive objectives are used. They include components of discovery learning (student-centered growth), constructivism (building of new meaning), and reception learning (structured learning)	7	
Humanistic objectives are used. They include components of individualization (student-tailored instruction), affective education (values training), and intrinsic learning (learning for its own sake)	7	
A combination of behavioral, cognitive, and humanistic learning objectives are used for technology-related lessons. Criteria for successful student learning are readily identified	7	
Your Score (7 possible)	➡	

ITEM 17—TECHNOLOGY-BASED LEARNING OBJECTIVES

Purpose of the Question

This question addresses preparation for behavioral, cognitive, or humanistic learning. Developing specific, observable, measurable, and attainable learning objectives is more an art than a science, requiring frequent revision as students and content material evolve. This question awards as many as 7 points toward the development of technology-based learning objectives based on sound principles of educational psychology.

Justification for Points Awarded

Learning objectives are not identifiable in classroom lesson plans (0 points).   Research has found that successful teachers prepare their own technology-based learning objectives for classroom instruction. Teachers who do not explicitly define student learning outcomes cannot possibly know when those skills have been mastered. No points are awarded for this response.

Learning objectives are used for technology-related lessons, but it is difficult to identify any criteria for successful student learning (1 point).   One point is awarded for a good faith attempt to document technology-based learning. Be on the lookout for weak objectives that typically omit the descriptive standards that indicate successful learning.

Behavioral objectives are used (7 points).   Teachers who prefer behavioral learning objectives assume that all student behavior is a response to their environment and that all behavior is learned. As a result, any behavior is analyzed in terms of its reinforcement history. According to the behaviorist, the ultimate teacher responsibility, and the only reason to bestow the full 7 points for this response, is to construct a technology environment in which the probability of reinforcing "correct" or proper student behavior is maximized. This goal is best attained by careful organization and presentation of information in a logical sequence.

Cognitive objectives are used (7 points).   Cognitive teachers focus on the student as an active participant in the teaching–learning process. Those who adhere to this psychology of learning and receive the full 7 points believe that teachers are more effective if they know what prior knowledge the student already possesses and how information was constructed. Cognitive teachers use teaching strategies that help the learner acquire knowledge more effectively and use technology to assist in this endeavor.

Humanistic objectives are used (7 points).   Humanistic teachers believe that how a person feels about learning is as important as how the person thinks or behaves. They describe behavior not from the viewpoint of the teacher, but from that of the student. The humanist teacher centers on learning objectives that foster self-development, cooperation, positive communications, and personalization of information and merits the full 7 points for this response.

A combination of behavioral, cognitive, and humanistic learning objectives are used for technology-related lessons (7 points).   A teacher who truly understands learning theory and instructional technology also understands that a single learning style unduly restricts student learning opportunities and limits the effectiveness of technology as an instructional strategy. Seven points are awarded if the teacher offers a blend of objectives for his or her classroom and students.

Issues to Consider When Assessing This Item

- Behavioral learning objectives include actions to be performed (behavior), the specific tools for learning to be used during the lesson (condition), and an assessment to gauge successful learning outcomes (criteria). Instructional applications of behavioristic learning include the following:
  - *Programmed instruction,* a self-paced instructional package that presents a topic in a carefully planned sequence and requires the learner to respond to questions or statements by filling in blanks, selecting from a series of answers, or solving a problem. Immediate feedback occurs after each response, and students work at their own pace.
  - *Computer-assisted instruction (CAI)* makes use of computer programs as the primary teaching tool. CAI presents information, gives students the opportunity to practice what they learn, and provides additional instruction when required. CAI programs serve three basic functions in schools: drill and practice, simulations, and tutorials.
  - *Mastery learning* assumes that all students are able to learn what is taught if the instruction is approached systematically, if students are helped when they have difficulty, if they are given sufficient time to achieve mastery, and if there is some clear criterion of what constitutes mastery.

- Cognitive learning objectives include components of student-centered learning, constructivism, and structured teaching. Instructional applications of cognitive learning include the following:
  - *Discovery learning* offers students a process of inquiry with the teacher as a primary resource to ascertain the particular principle hidden in the lesson objective. The teacher must carefully plan the questions to help students understand the concepts, order the examples from simple to complex, and ensure that required reference materials and equipment are available for the asking.

- *Reception learning* encourages teachers to present material in a carefully organized, sequenced, and completed form. Students receive materials as required and progress deductively from the general to the specific.
- *Information processing* views learning from a computer-model perspective. Like the computer, the human mind takes in information, performs operations to change its form and content, stores the information, retrieves it when needed, and generates responses.

- Humanistic learning objectives include components of individualization (personalized instruction), affective education (values training), and intrinsic learning (learning for its own sake). Instructional applications of humanistic learning include the following:
  - *Open education* encompasses themes of humaneness, respect, and warmth, diagnosis of learning events, professional growth of student and teacher, and a warm and accepting learning environment.
  - *Cooperative learning* offers basic elements of positive interdependence, face-to-face interaction, individual accountability, collaborative skills, and group processing.

Recommendations for Increasing the Points Awarded

1. Create behavioral learning objectives with an observable behavior, specific classroom conditions, and measurable criteria of student success. For teachers who favor behavioral lessons, integrate technology into programmed instruction, computer-assisted instruction, and mastery learning lessons.

2. Create cognitive learning objectives with components of student-centered learning activities, constructivism, and structured teaching. For teachers who favor cognitive lessons, integrate technology into discovery learning, reception learning, and information processing lessons.

3. Create humanistic learning objectives by considering individualization, affective education, and intrinsic learning. For teachers who favor humanistic lessons, integrate technology into open education and cooperative learning lessons.

BIBLIOGRAPHY

Kemp, Jerrold E., Ross, Steven M., and Morrison, Gary R. *Designing Effective Instruction*, 3rd ed. New York: John Wiley & Sons, 2000.

Appendix 9.1

Scope and Sequence of Technology Skills K–12

Kindergarten: Appropriate Technology Skills

WORD-PROCESSING
Use a word processor in real world context

FUNDAMENTAL COMPUTER SKILLS
Use and understand basic computer-related terms

Identify basic computer hardware components and peripheral devices

Demonstrate care and appropriate use of hardware

Use basic computer management skills

COMPUTER NETWORKING AND TELECOMMUNICATION SKILLS
Use the network by demonstrating use of log-in numbers/names

LEGAL/ETHICAL SKILLS
Demonstrate appropriate computer etiquette

Grades 1–2: Appropriate Technology Skills

WORD-PROCESSING SKILLS
Create and save a new document

Open, view, and print documents

Format documents

Use a word processor in real-world context

FUNDAMENTAL COMPUTER SKILLS
Use and understand basic computer-related terms

Identify basic computer hardware components and peripheral devices

Identify the functions and advantages of computer-productivity software

COMPUTER NETWORKING AND TELECOMMUNICATION SKILLS
Use the network by demonstrating use of log-in numbers/names

Use the network by demonstrating use of network printing

LEGAL/ETHICAL SKILLS
Show understanding of appropriate legal/ethical conduct

Grades 3–4: Appropriate Technology Skills

WORD-PROCESSING SKILLS

Create and save a new document

Open, view, and print documents

Format documents

Edit text

Use desktop publishing techniques

Use a word processor in real-world context

FUNDAMENTAL COMPUTER SKILLS

Use and understand basic computer-related terms

Identify basic computer hardware components and peripheral devices

Demonstrate care and appropriate use of hardware

Use basic computer management skills

COMPUTER NETWORKING AND TELECOMMUNICATION SKILLS

Use the network by sending and receiving electronic mail

Use the network by accessing online information for research

LEGAL/ETHICAL SKILLS

Demonstrate legal/ethical conduct by respecting the privacy of all users

Understand appropriate legal/ethical conduct by obeying copyright laws

INFORMATION MANAGEMENT SKILLS

Access/retrieve information

Organize information

Identify useful information from search

Grades 5–6: Appropriate Technology Skills

WORD-PROCESSING SKILLS

Create and save a new document

Open, view, and print documents

Format documents

Edit text

Use desktop publishing techniques

Use a word processor in real-world context

FUNDAMENTAL COMPUTER SKILLS
Use and understand basic computer-related terms
Identify basic computer hardware components and peripheral devices
Demonstrate care and appropriate use of hardware
Identify the functions and advantages of computer-productivity software
Use basic computer management skills

COMPUTER NETWORKING AND TELECOMMUNICATION SKILLS
Use the network by sending and receiving electronic mail
Use the network by setting up user passwords
Use the network by accessing online information for research

LEGAL/ETHICAL SKILLS
Demonstrate legal/ethical conduct by respecting the privacy of all users
Understand appropriate legal/ethical conduct by obeying copyright laws

INFORMATION MANAGEMENT SKILLS
Use of library catalog
Use of commercial database
Organize information
Information analysis

Grades 7–8: Appropriate Technology Skills

WORD-PROCESSING SKILLS
Format documents
Use desktop publishing techniques
Use a word processor in real-world context

FUNDAMENTAL COMPUTER SKILLS
Identify basic computer hardware components and peripheral devices
Care and appropriate use of hardware
Identify the functions and advantages of computer-productivity software
Use basic computer management skills

COMPUTER NETWORKING AND TELECOMMUNICATION SKILLS
Use the network by sending and receiving electronic mail
Use the network by changing user passwords

LEGAL/ETHICAL SKILLS
Demonstrate legal/ethical conduct by respecting the privacy of all users
Understand appropriate legal/ethical conduct by obeying copyright laws

INFORMATION MANAGEMENT SKILLS
Use library catalog
Use commercial database
Use student-created database
Use Internet
Organize information
Analyze information

DATABASE SKILLS
Create and save databases
Retrieve data
Edit data

SPREADSHEET SKILLS
Create and save spreadsheets
Retrieve data
Edit data
Generate graphs from spreadsheets

High School Grades 9–12: Appropriate Technology Skills

WORD-PROCESSING SKILLS
Format documents
Edit text
Use desktop publishing techniques
Use a word processor in real-world context

FUNDAMENTAL COMPUTER SKILLS
Identify basic computer hardware components and peripheral devices
Demonstrate care and appropriate use of hardware
Identify the functions and advantages of computer-productivity software
Use basic computer management skills

COMPUTER NETWORKING AND TELECOMMUNICATION SKILLS
Use the network by sending and receiving electronic mail

Use the network via multiple storage drives

Use the network by saving files to individual home directories

LEGAL/ETHICAL SKILLS

Demonstrate legal/ethical conduct by respecting the privacy of all users

Understand appropriate legal/ethical conduct by obeying copyright laws

INFORMATION MANAGEMENT SKILLS

Use library catalog

Use commercial database

Use student-created database

Use Internet

Organize information

Analyze information

DATABASE SKILLS

Create and save databases

Retrieve data

Edit data

SPREADSHEET SKILLS

Create and save spreadsheets

Retrieve data

Edit data

Generate graphs from spreadsheets

CHAPTER 10

PLANNING THE INTEGRATION OF TECHNOLOGY

Section I: Planning the Lesson and the Technologies

Continuing with the Kemp ISD model, this chapter focuses on Steps 6 and 7 of *Designing Effective Instruction*. Step 6 focuses on the teacher's effort to plan the lesson and offers progressive stages for creating the materials required for the lesson. Step 7 encourages the teacher to plan for the technology by selecting from among various systems of computers, video, audio, multimedia, and so on. Together, Steps 6 and 7 represent planning for the integration of technology.

STEP 6: DESIGN THE INSTRUCTIONAL STRATEGIES AND MATERIALS

In this step, teachers complete the design phase of lesson development by selecting the most appropriate strategies for classroom delivery and locate, or create themselves, the materials for student learning.

Key characteristics.   Examine each element in the lesson sequence. Identify the most promising strategies for teaching the element, along with any prerequisite student skills, practical classroom issues, and required outside assistance. Also describe the consequences of not mastering each element.

Teacher's task.   Develop the instructional requirements and appropriate student materials. Technology-based media are tailored specifically to student needs, interests, and capabilities. Research indicates that by collecting, revising, and consolidating resources, teachers produce better instructional materials than those in commercially-prepared packages.

For integrating technology into the curriculum, three popular formats are demonstrated in this chapter. Text-based materials use features of word processing to produce individualized student handouts, study guides, and workbooks. Visual-based materials present on-screen slide shows, overhead transparencies, and hard copy notes to enhance student learning. Web-based materials consider student age, maturity level, and technical competence when creating personalized lesson home pages.

Examples of the three formats are provided in Appendixes 10.1 through 10.3 for further examination. The reader may learn more about developing these classroom resources from *Teaching Digitally in the 21st Century* (Tomei, 2001) which explicitly aids the classroom teacher in the step-by-step development of technology-based, student-centered resources.

Creating the Text-Based Workbook

A example workbook based on a fourth-grade lesson about dinosaurs is included in Appendix 10.1 at the end of this chapter. It depicts the proper construction of text-based resources, which include the following elements:

■ *Cover page.* The first page contains the title of the workbook and an image, perhaps taken from a web site, depicting the theme of the lesson.

■ *Indicative data and instructions.* Because the workbook belongs to the student, it should begin with the student's name, date of the lesson, and the teacher's name. Instructions are particularly important for students who will use the workbook in a self-paced approach or in a team environment.

■ *Lesson goals.* A workbook should contain no more than two to four individual lesson objectives. Behavioral, cognitive, or humanistic objectives should appear verbatim in the workbook to promote student understanding. At least one of the objectives should be a required, hands-on, realistic activity that permits the student to explore and personalize the knowledge and skills taught.

■ *Self-evaluation.* The workbook should include several questions to encourage student feedback regarding the lesson. Make the questions short, and allow for short answer responses, not just multiple choice.

■ *Interactive page(s).* Complete the workbook with exercises taken directly from web sites; make them available for students to tear out, color, and post on the class bulletin board. Construct the pages with additional information to enhance learning. This recommendation is most appropriate for grades K–6, but if used discreetly, these pages increase understanding at all levels.

Creating the Visual-Based Presentation

An example slide presentation in Appendix 10.2 demonstrates the construction of visual-based resources. Elements include the following:

■ *Opening slide.* Similar to a workbook cover page, the opening slide contains the title of the presentation and an image depicting the theme of the lesson.

■ *Introductory slide.* Also known as a topic slide, this screen restates the title of the lesson and displays the major topics for presentation.

■ *Learning objectives.* A visual-based presentation should contain two to six individual lesson objectives, primarily concrete, behavioral objectives. Multimedia tools make the presentation more concrete; consider using sound clips, sound files, clip art, images, and video clips. The hyperlink connects one document to another or connects the student to web sites preselected by the teacher.

■ *Formative and summative assessment.* One of the advantages of the visual presentation format is the ease of assessment. Formative assessment examines the student's ongoing understanding of the content material. Online help is provided if there is a problem with comprehension. Summative assessment comes at the end of the lesson and measures overall student achievement. Slides 11 and 12 in the example presentation demonstrate the characteristics of online assessment.

■ *Interactive online explorations.* One of the final slides offers the student an opportunity to explore new materials via the World Wide Web. Hyperlinks offer students additional content validated by the teacher for easy access and appropriate application.

Creating the Web-Based Course Page

An example of a web-based course page is shown in Appendix 10.3. When properly constructed, course pages host the following key elements below:

■ *Opening screen.* The opening screen has an initial image taken from the lesson.

■ *Introduction.* A course page begins with a general overview. A short prologue sets the stage for the reader and is appropriate for any grade level.

■ *Instructions.* Keep the instructions simple, and do not assume that all students understand how to navigate the site. A previous lesson on the use of Internet browsers is recommended.

■ *Learning objectives.* Confine a course page to no more than four learning objectives, predominantly combined with significant multimedia material. Designers often use too much multimedia simply because it is available, which actually detracts from the learning. As with text-based and visual-based formats, do not shy away from specifying the exact learning objective; students prefer to know what must be done to complete the task at hand.

■ *Web sites for personal exploration.* A well-designed course page includes additional links for individual student exploration. Review all sites for content, ease of access, and freedom from inappropriate material. Do not use search engines with K–6 students. Use both internal and external links. An internal link connects the student to other teacher-made web pages. For example, the "Instructions" screen at the end of Appendix 10.3 is an internal link that offers the student additional guidance for completing the lesson. But of course, it requires extra work on the part of the teacher. An external link connects to a Web page elsewhere on the Internet. Excellent sites have already been created for the Holocaust, dinosaurs, and even the Pythagorean theorem. Why reinvent the wheel?

■ *Student assessment criteria.* A well-constructed course page includes a legend explaining the available points for the project and how the points contribute to a final letter grade.

■ *Address block.* The address block is standard on all well-designed course pages placed on a school's site. The block contains indicative data such as the name and contact information of the page designer, course information, an email address for the school (avoid student or teacher email addresses), a fair use statement, and a created and revised date for copyright purposes.

STEP 7: SELECT THE APPROPRIATE INSTRUCTIONAL TECHNOLOGY

Deciding on the actual delivery techniques for the instruction occurs relatively late in the instructional system design phase. But no step in the Kemp model of instructional design is more important.

Key characteristics.   Delivering technology-enhanced instruction is not that different from other models of classroom presentation. Table 10.1 offers six of the most popular technologies used for teaching. Classroom computers, lab computers, audio, visual, audiovisual, and noncomputer labs represent the wide range of available technology. Each is synchronized with lesson characteristics that aid the teacher in matching technology to teaching style. The chart shows an X in each cell where the medium is most appropriate to lesson criteria. Select instructional technology accordingly.

Teacher's task.   Prepare to conduct the lesson using specific technologies that enhance the learning experience. Technology must become another instructional strategy. For many teachers, the following paradigm aids in preparing a successful lesson.

- *Ready yourself.* Review the content and the possible applications of technology. Teachers must have a thorough knowledge of the academic content and understand the strengths and weaknesses of the available technologies.
- *Ready the classroom.* Preparation and testing of the technology is crucial; the physical environment of the classroom must contribute to the effectiveness of the technology to be employed.
- *Practice the technology—and prepare a backup.* Schedule the technology (e.g., computer lab, multimedia cart, etc.). Prepare the instructional materials (reproduce workbooks, copy diskettes, distribute copies of slides). Test the technology—twice.
- *Ready the audience.* The most critical step in the delivery of instruction is the preparation of students to learn. Students should always know what they are expected to learn and how the technology will aid in that endeavor.
- *Present the lesson using the technology.* A well-planned lesson is delivered with confidence. Teachers who know how to troubleshoot technology transition easily into a nontechnical version of the lesson should disaster strike.
- *Follow up the lesson with other learning activities.* A viable instructional strategy demands that technology is used as part of an overall curriculum of learning. Some of the most important and successful classroom learning involves integrating technology with other learning activities.

Section II recognizes that teachers in the twenty-first century will be expected to successfully integrate technology-based objectives into their curriculums. Questions 18 and 19 explore the extent of those applications in the classroom and the current scheduling situation in the school.

TABLE 10.1 Instructional Technology Characteristics

LESSON CHARACTERISTICS	CLASSROOM COMPUTERS	LAB COMPUTERS	AUDIO	VIDEO	AUDIOVISUAL	LABS	OTHER
Group Size							
Large (> 30)			X	X	X		
Medium						X	
Small (< 12)	X	X					
Individual	X	X					
Technical Challenge							
High	X	X					
Medium			X	X	X	X	
Low							
Time Constraints							
< 1 Period	X	X					
1 Period					X	X	
> 1 Period			X	X			
Media Format							
Text-based	X				X	X	
Visual-based	X	X		X		X	
Web-based	X	X					
Cost							
Expensive	X	X		X	X	X	
Affordable				X			
Inexpensive			X			X	
Pacing							
Fixed			X	X			
Flexible	X		X		X	X	

LESSON CHARACTERISTICS	CLASSROOM COMPUTERS	LAB COMPUTERS	AUDIO	VIDEO	AUDIOVISUAL	LABS	OTHER
Learner Strengths							
Concrete	X	X			X		
Abstract	X	X	X	X	X	X	
Learner Challenges							
Describe							
Describe							
Required for Lesson Success							
Optional	X	X	X				
Suggested				X		X	
Required					X		
Availability							
Local	X	X			X		
Off-site			X	X		X	
Production							
Teacher-made	X	X	X				
Media-made				X	X	X	
Schedule							
Insert Date							
Experience							
Prior use			X	X	X		
First-time use	X	X				X	

Section II: Technology Facade Checklist Items 18 and 19

18. When using technology-based lessons in the classroom, which of the following resources do teachers personally develop and use for instruction? Identify all that apply.

	Points Available	Points Awarded
Text-based materials such as handouts, study guides, and workbooks to guide the lesson	5	
Visual-based presentations, including overhead transparencies to support classroom instruction	5	
Web-based course pages for student exploration and cooperative learning	5	
Your Score (15 possible)	➡	

ITEM 18—TEACHER-DEVELOPED RESOURCES

Purpose of the Question

Students are best served when technology is tailored to the instruction at hand, rather than the instruction modified to fit available commercial media. To accomplish this task, teachers must learn to create their own text, visual, and web-based materials. This item offers 15 points for teachers who personalize materials for their students. Five points are awarded for text-based materials such as handouts, study guides, and workbooks. Another 5 points are available for visual-based materials that integrate images, sounds, and clip art graphics. And 5 more points are given for integrating web-based materials such as course pages.

Justification for Points Awarded

Text-based materials such as handouts, study guides, and workbooks to guide the lesson (5 points).   Teachers who prepare text-based materials are awarded up to 5 points if the materials are age appropriate, tested and validated under classroom conditions, and contain the minimum elements described earlier. To receive all 5 points, the teacher must also be willing to share these materials with other educators.

Visual-based presentations, including overhead transparencies to support classroom instruction (5 points).   To receive up to 5 points, a visual-based presentation should contain the minimum slides described earlier, plus the materials must be age appropriate and tested and validated under classroom conditions. As with the previous category, to receive all 5 points, the teacher must be willing to share these materials with other educators.

Web-based course pages for student exploration and cooperative learning (5 points).   Web pages make excellent teacher-made lessons. With so many resources already available on the Internet, teachers who master the design of web pages for instruction lead their schools in the twenty-first century. To receive points, all web-based materials must be age appropriate, tested and validated under classroom conditions, and created using nonprogramming technology. In other words, the pages must be created using tools made available to the teacher by school administration; absolutely no additional points are given for using Java scripting, HTML language, or sophisticated web development packages that cost thousands of dollars. The simpler, the better, in this category. Again, the teacher must be willing to share these materials with other educators.

Issues to Consider When Assessing This Item

- In addition to the pedagogical benefits associated with abstract concepts, teachers need concrete, hard copy resources and a viable assessment tool for use after the online session is concluded.
- Student *handouts* provide instructions, definitions, rubrics, comments, hypotheses and theories, worksheets, maps, comments, data sheets, design sheets, lesson layouts, and more. They assist teachers with a collection of materials, online information, lessons and activities, concrete representations, ideas, resources and instructions, safety tips, and discovery procedures.
- *Study guides* provide students with a table of contents, study quizzes, links to related web sites, course information, course outlines, learning objectives, chapter objectives, instructional resources, and textbook reading guides. They assist teachers with important concepts captured from film, history, images, media, music, news, television, and the Internet.
- *Workbooks* address explicit learning objectives and content materials. They are more comprehensive than either handouts or study guides,

and they include areas of student assessment and self-discovery not typically found in less-comprehensive materials.

■ *Slides* offer pictures, movies, and charts; automatic graphics and sound; on-screen slide shows or overhead projections; hard copy printing of slides and handouts; and customized backgrounds, clip art, inserted images, and drawing tools.

■ *Overhead transparencies* are more transportable for the educator, who may be using the materials in front of a fifth-grade class on Tuesday and as a guest speaker at a national seminar the following weekend. They also provide an excellent backup in case of technology failure. Visual-based materials include transparencies, videotape, filmstrips, and 35-mm slides.

■ *Course pages* are the future of teaching and learning. The Internet contains literally hundreds of thousands of sites, yet there are many limitations. For example, much of the material is inappropriate for certain content areas; some is unsuitable for school-age children; and still other material is incompatible with a teacher's specific learning objectives.

■ If instructional technology is to reach its full potential as a teaching and learning strategy, educators must come to know and understand not only how to find text-, visual-, and web-based resources, but how to create them as well.

Recommendations for Increasing the Points Awarded

1. Use handouts, study guides, and workbooks to teach theories and concepts, provide students with hard copy resources, and conduct realistic assessments of student understanding.

2. Use slide presentations and overhead transparencies to incorporate pictures, movies, charts, graphics, and sound. Use on-screen slide shows, overhead projections, or hard copy of slides for classroom presentation and student resources.

3. Design course pages to overcome the limitations of the Internet. Consider grade and age levels, student maturity, and compatibility with your own learning objectives. Appreciate the Internet's potential as a teaching and learning strategy. Read educational technology journals. Participate in formal seminars, conferences, and professional symposiums. And enroll in formal technology programs to increase your use of instructional technology.

19. Describe what typically happens when classroom teachers wish to use technology resources to present a lesson. Select one.

	Points Available	Points Awarded
The computer labs or technology resources are often unavailable	0	
The technology teacher or coordinator must present the lesson	1	
Technology must be transported into the classroom for the session	3	
Computer labs or technology resources are available for scheduling without significant delays	5	
Your Score (5 possible)	➡	

ITEM 19—AVAILABILITY OF TECHNOLOGY RESOURCES

Purpose of the Question

Availability of resources is an important predictor of how quickly a teacher might adopt technology for the classroom. Without proper training, it is often the case that the technology coordinator must step in to conduct the session. If teachers are expected to search out a multimedia cart, replace burned out projection bulbs, or diagnose severely malfunctioning equipment, odds are they will abandon that technology the next time. If, on the other hand, scheduling the lab is aided by a real-time calendar and a competent facilitator, if training is available on demand before a technology is to be put into practice, and if the equipment is maintained in good working order, a school's technology program thrives.

Justification for Points Awarded

The computer labs or technology resources are often unavailable (0 points). No points are awarded if teachers must routinely fight for technology. Unavailability suggests insufficient quantities of equipment, a lack of quality equipment, misplaced technology, or school policies that dissuade its use.

The technology teacher or coordinator must present the lesson (1 point). To receive points, a school must already have a technology teacher or coordinator; therefore, points have already been awarded in a previous Checklist item. Only 1 point is awarded here because the teacher should become self-sufficient with respect to technology as quickly as possible.

Technology must be transported into the classroom for the session (3 points). Transporting technology around the school is nothing to be ashamed of. If classroom learning is achieved with a single laptop computer on a multimedia cart, outfitting an entire computer lab is not fiscally responsible. Three points are awarded if moving technology is both appropriate and effective. However, transporting equipment in lieu of a reasonable quantity of technology results in no points. If there is still not enough media even after carts are added to the school's inventory, do not award any points.

Computer labs or technology resources are available for scheduling without significant delays (5 points).   Teachers do not expect immediate access to technology and should not be annoyed if a lesson must be delayed for a few days because they forgot to schedule the computer lab. Also, students should not feel learning is compromised because they must share computers. Five points are given if schools properly balance their technology resources.

Issues to Consider When Assessing This Item

- Limited technology is best maintained in a centralized location providing easy access for teachers and physical security for the equipment.
- A system for reporting malfunctioning hardware and software ensures that equipment is quickly replaced with working substitutes.
- Teachers should be trained in both the operation and routine maintenance of classroom technology.
- The technology coordinator should be present the first time a teacher uses a particular technology. Thereafter, the teacher should understand that use of the technology comes without further assistance.
- Software packages are available to monitor the status of all school technology, including maintenance and scheduling. One popular package schedules up to 400 categories in 24-hour-a-day increments as small as 10 minutes. It prints confirmations and offers optional password protection. Another scheduling package generates service requests and routes them to the technology coordinator.
- Multimedia carts are excellent tools for the classroom if they hold a laptop computer, projector, audiovisual media, and Internet connectivity.
- Educational software for teacher check-out is an important instructional technology for schools and classrooms.
- Separate technology labs and computer classrooms are helpful. Computer classrooms are set aside for teacher presentations and should be restricted to single-period time slots and scheduled at least 1 week in advance so that the technology coordinator can prepare the facility. Technology labs should be open and available to both teachers and students throughout the academic day and after school.

Recommendations for Increasing the Points Awarded

1. Ensure that there are sufficient technology resources for all students. Request assistance from the school's Technology Committee when planning the quantity and quality of the technologies.

2. Do not overextend the school's budget on large capital outlays (e.g., computer labs) when smaller quantities of technology are just as effective. One multimedia cart, equipped with a laptop computer and projector, is also a viable classroom technology.

3. Maintain limited technology resources in a centralized location. If possible, assign a media staff member to preposition the equipment in classrooms before school begins in the morning, during lunch periods, or during free periods. Ensure the physical security of the equipment at all times.

4. Establish a reporting system for malfunctioning hardware and software, and reserve a reasonable number of working spares in case of emergency. Do not allow the computer technician, network administrator, or technology coordinator to maintain a "cannibal closet" of parts and pieces taken from already nonworking technologies to repair other nonworking technologies.

5. Train teachers in the basic operation and maintenance of all technology used in the classroom.

6. The coordinator may be present the first time a teacher uses a particular technology to assist with problems and ease the integration into the curriculum. After that initial introduction, it must be clear that technology is the teacher's responsibility.

7. Select a commercially available software package to monitor the status of technology, recurring or periodic maintenance, and classroom scheduling.

8. Use carts to transport technology throughout the school. A workable multimedia cart includes a computer, projector, video player, and Internet connectivity.

9. Maintain and account for educational software in the school library.

10. Distinguish between a technology lab and a computer classroom. The technology lab must be open during the school day for teachers and students. Computer classrooms, however, are restricted to single-period classroom presentations and must be scheduled well before a planned lesson.

BIBLIOGRAPHY

Kemp, Jerrold E., Ross, Steven M., and Morrison, Gary R. *Designing Effective Instruction*, 3rd ed. New York: John Wiley & Sons, 2000.

Tomei, Lawrence A. *Teaching Digitally: A Guide for Integrating Technology into the Curriculum.* Norwood, MA: Christopher-Gordon Publishing, 2001.

Appendix 10.1
The Dinosaur Workbook

I. COVER PAGE

The Dinosaur Workbook
Dinosaurs of North America

II. INDICATIVE DATA AND INSTRUCTIONS

Student Name: _____

Date of the Lesson: _____

Teacher: _____

Instructions: Each fourth-grade student will receive his or her own copy of this student workbook. At this point in the third semester of the school year, you are encouraged to explore the subject of this lesson with other members of your class. For this particular lesson, your significant experience with group work is as important as the material you will be studying.

You already know quite a lot about dinosaurs. The class has watched several dinosaur movies in our classroom and read at least two books checked out of the school library. You should know something about the United States as well, and the area of the country where dinosaur fossils are most commonly found, since we finished our geography chapter on states of the Midwest last week. You have also been on the Internet at least three times in computer class, so you should know how to point and click a link to access a web site.

Explore the subject at your own pace and in keeping with your own personal learning goals. The questions being asked are designed to guide you through the lesson objectives to ensure that you experience the full range of goals and performance objectives targeted by your teacher. You do not have to complete the questions in the order they are presented. But you should complete **all** of the questions.

Be sure to turn in all of the material requested to your teacher. If at any time you encounter difficulty, immediately notify your teacher and the facilitator of the exploration.

III. LESSON GOALS

1. Examine the DinoPages and draw a circle around your favorite creature.

Explain why this is your favorite dinosaur on the lines below.

_____

_____

_____

2. Find another dinosaur that is not in this workbook by accessing the following web site: **http://www.enchantedlearning.com/subjects/dinosaurs/ dinos/dinolist.html** When you decide on which creature you like the best, complete the information below. Your teacher will help you use the computer to find the site.

a. Describe the dinosaur (its anatomy and size)

_____

_____

_____

b. Was the dinosaur an omnivore or carnivore? What did it eat?

_____

_____

_____

c. Draw your dinosaur in the box below.

IV. SELF-EVALUATION

3. Please evaluate this lesson on dinosaurs. Circle your answer.
   Yes / No   a. Did you enjoy using computers to find dinosaurs?

Yes / No   b. Did you discover information about dinosaurs that you did not know before? If so, please name at least one or two new things you learned.

_____

_____

c. What is your experience as a computer user? Check one.

_____ I have a computer at home and can get to the Internet.

_____ I have a computer at home but have never used the Internet.

_____ I want a computer for Christmas!

_____ I use a computer only at school.

V. INTERACTIVE PAGE(S)

DinoPage 1

**Tyrannosaurus Rex:
The Tyrant Lizard King**

Anatomy

Tyrannosaurus rex was a fierce predator that walked on two powerful legs in Cretaceous period forests. This meat-eater had a huge head with large, pointed, replaceable teeth and well-developed jaw muscles. It had tiny arms, each with two fingers. Each bird-like foot had three large toes, all equipped with claws. T. rex had a slim, stiff, pointed tail that provided balance and allowed quick turns while running. T. rex's neck was short and muscular. Its body was solidly built but its bones were hollow. T. rex's jaws were up to 4 feet (1.2 m) long and had 50 to 60 thick, conical, bone-crunching teeth that were up to 9 inches (23 cm) long. T. rex could eat 500 pounds (230 kg) of meat and bones in one bite! T. rex had a wrap-around overbite; when T. rex closed its mouth, the upper parts of the lower jaw's teeth fit inside the lower jaw.

Size

Tyrannosaurus rex was up to 40 feet (12.4 m) long, about 15 to 20 feet (4.6 to 6 m) tall. It was roughly 5 to 7 tons in weight. T. rex left footprints 1.55 feet (46 cm) long (although its feet were much longer, about 3.3 feet (1 m) long, T. rex, like other dinosaurs walked on its toes).

Other Huge Meat-Eating Dinosaurs

Although not the biggest meat-eating dinosaur ever discovered, Tyrannosaurus rex was certainly one of the largest terrestrial carnivores of all time. The recently discovered Giganotosaurus carolinii and Carcharodontosaurus may have been even more enormous.

DinoPage 2

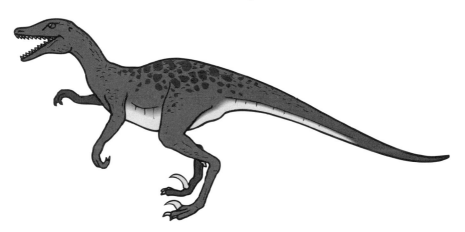

Velociraptor: The Speedy Thief

Anatomy

Velociraptor was a speedy, bipedal carnivore. It had about 30 very sharp, curved teeth in a long, flat snout, an s-shaped neck, long thin legs, arms with three-fingered clawed hands, and four-toed clawed feet. Velociraptor may have been able to run up to roughly 40 mph (60 km/hr) for short bursts. Velociraptor was about 6 feet long (2 m), and 3 feet tall (1 m). It may have weighed about 15 to 33 pounds (7 to 15 kg). It had a stiff tail that worked as a counterbalance and let it make very quick turns. One 7 inch (18 cm) long, sickle-like, retractable claw was on the middle toes of each foot. This claw was its main weapon, and could probably kill most of its prey easily. Velociraptor brains were very large in comparison to their body size (this is true for all the Dromaeosaurid dinosaurs, who were the most intelligent dinosaurs).

Behavior

Velociraptor may have hunted in packs, attacking even very large animals. In 1971, fossils of a Velociraptor and a Protoceratops were found together. They died together; the Velociraptor was attacking the Protoceratops with its claws and the armored head of the Protoceratops had apparently pierced the chest of the Velociraptor. Velociraptor, along with the other Dromaeosaurids, were the smartest dinosaurs, as calculated from their brain:body weight ratio. This made them very deadly predators.

Appendix 10.2

The Dinosaur Visual-Based Presentation

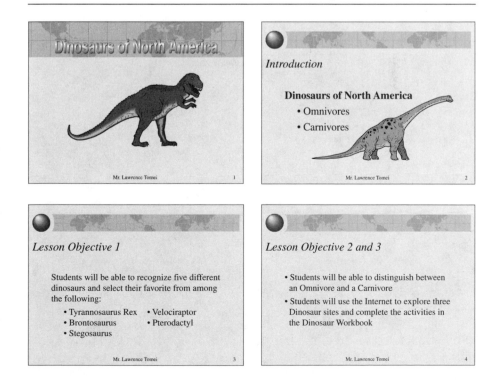

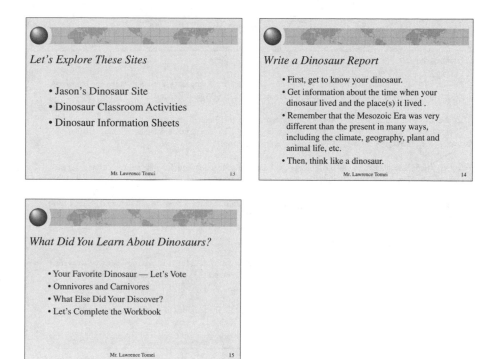

Let's Explore These Sites

- Jason's Dinosaur Site
- Dinosaur Classroom Activities
- Dinosaur Information Sheets

Mr. Lawrence Tomei   13

Write a Dinosaur Report

- First, get to know your dinosaur.
- Get information about the time when your dinosaur lived and the place(s) it lived .
- Remember that the Mesozoic Era was very different than the present in many ways, including the climate, geography, plant and animal life, etc.
- Then, think like a dinosaur.

Mr. Lawrence Tomei   14

What Did You Learn About Dinosaurs?

- Your Favorite Dinosaur — Let's Vote
- Omnivores and Carnivores
- What Else Did Your Discover?
- Let's Complete the Workbook

Mr. Lawrence Tomei   15

Appendix 10.3

The Dinosaur Web Course Page

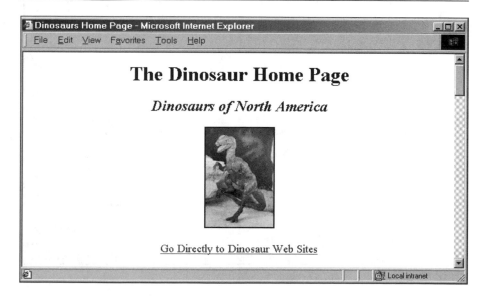

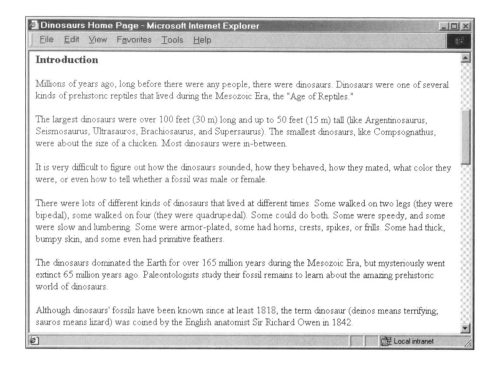

Introduction

Millions of years ago, long before there were any people, there were dinosaurs. Dinosaurs were one of several kinds of prehistoric reptiles that lived during the Mesozoic Era, the "Age of Reptiles."

The largest dinosaurs were over 100 feet (30 m) long and up to 50 feet (15 m) tall (like Argentinosaurus, Seismosaurus, Ultrasauros, Brachiosaurus, and Supersaurus). The smallest dinosaurs, like Compsognathus, were about the size of a chicken. Most dinosaurs were in-between.

It is very difficult to figure out how the dinosaurs sounded, how they behaved, how they mated, what color they were, or even how to tell whether a fossil was male or female.

There were lots of different kinds of dinosaurs that lived at different times. Some walked on two legs (they were bipedal), some walked on four (they were quadrupedal). Some could do both. Some were speedy, and some were slow and lumbering. Some were armor-plated, some had horns, crests, spikes, or frills. Some had thick, bumpy skin, and some even had primitive feathers.

The dinosaurs dominated the Earth for over 165 million years during the Mesozoic Era, but mysteriously went extinct 65 million years ago. Paleontologists study their fossil remains to learn about the amazing prehistoric world of dinosaurs.

Although dinosaurs' fossils have been known since at least 1818, the term dinosaur (deinos means terrifying; sauros means lizard) was coined by the English anatomist Sir Richard Owen in 1842.

Instructions

Read the instructions for completing this lesson and the companion Workbook and Slide Presentation by clicking on this icon.

Lesson Objectives

Objective I: Using a personal computer and Web address list, students will **navigate** the Internet locating two specific Dinosaur Web sites and, **locate, download, and print** at least two images of your favorite dinosaurs.

Objective II: After locating a given **Web** site, a student will review the information and answer the questions in the **Workbook**: "*What is the difference between an Omnivores and a Carnivore? When did the Dinosaurs Live? And, What Where the Most Common Dinosaurs in North America?*"

Objective III: Given a Web address, students will click on a dinosaur's name to go to a simple black-and-white print-out and color, cut out, and mount their favorite Dinosaur. Students will share a **3-5 minute presentation** on their Favorite Dinosaur and discuss Why the Dinosaur is their favorite and WHY this lesson was important to them.

Dinosaurs Home Page - Microsoft Internet Explorer   `_ □ ×`

File   Edit   View   Favorites   Tools   Help

Web Sites for Student Exploration

The following Web Sites have been selected for this course. Examine each of the sites -- in order. If you have any trouble locating a site, please ask for assistance from your instructor.

- Jason's Dinosaur Site
- Dinosaur Classroom Activities
- Dinosaur Information Sheets and Print Outs
- Honolulu Community College Dinosaur Exhibit

Student Assessment. You will receive a grade for this lesson based on the following criteria.

Assessment	Possible Points	Percent of Points
Attendance and Participation	100 points	10%
Web Site Navigation	500 points	50%
Workbook	100 points	10%
Presentation	300 points	30%
Total Possible	**1000 points**	**100%**

Local intranet

Dinosaurs Home Page - Microsoft Internet Explorer   `_ □ ×`

File   Edit   View   Favorites   Tools   Help

Created and Maintained by Miss Tammy Brown
Email Address: brown@schoolwise.edu
5th Grade Science Teacher
Schoolwise Elementary School
Email Address: schoolwise@schoolwise.edu

Fair Use Statement
Permission is granted for unrestricted of the materials found on this Web Page. Author requests that any materials (text or images) acquired from these pages for inclusion in related resources carry a citation of the Author as indicated below.

Created: 10/01/99
Revised: 01/01/00

Local intranet

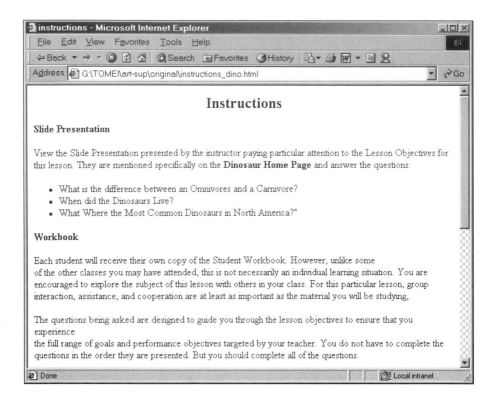

PLANNING FOR SUCCESSFUL LEARNING

Section I: Planning for Successful Learning

Completing the examination of the ISD model, Chapter 11 concentrates on the last two steps of Kemp's book, *Designing Effective Instruction.* It also offers a look at the predominant standards for key academic content areas that contribute to the assessment and selection of instructional materials and presents the final Checklist item for consideration. ISD Step 8 develops appropriate evaluation instruments and offers some key characteristics of reliable and valid assessment tools. ISD Step 9 helps the teacher choose the instructional materials (including technology resources) that best suit the lesson being developed.

STEP 8: DEVELOP EVALUATION INSTRUMENTS

Meaningful assessment demands two things: First, criteria against which the appraisal of student performance may be measured. Second, an accurate appraisal of student understanding that enables teachers to make appropriate instructional decisions. The first demand involves an appreciation of academic standards and is a matter for discussion as a key characteristic. The second demand requires a grasp of the theories of testing and measurement, and that is the responsibility of the classroom teacher.

Key characteristics.   Within the last 5 years, increased attention has been placed on the development and approval of standards for specific academic content areas, especially for the relatively new curricular area of technology. The International Society for Technology in Education (ISTE) recently published its comprehensive *National Educational Technology Standards for Students: Connecting Curriculum and Technology* (ISTE, 2000). Curriculum teams in English, language arts, foreign language, mathematics, science, and social studies—plus multidisciplinary teams focused on Pre-K–2, grades 3–5, grades 6–8, and grades 9–12—studied what seemed like every possible aspect of technology in the classroom to prepare this excellent tool for teachers considering the integration of technology into their curriculum. With such depth of content, this publication is recommended without reservation for Step 8 of any technology-based curriculum plan. To demonstrate the exhaustive coverage of these international standards, Table 11.1 represents select student performance criteria for preschool, elementary, and high school students.

In addition, as technology is integrated into the curriculum of all academic content areas, national councils are beginning to develop technology-

TABLE 11.1   Technology Performance Criteria—Grade Pre-K through Grade 12

PRE-K–2	GRADES 3–5	GRADES 6–8	GRADES 9–12
Use the mouse, keyboard, monitor, printer, and other computer peripherals.	Demonstrate knowledge of information technology and its trends in society and the workplace.	Solve routine hardware and software problems.	Identify advantages and limitations of emerging technologies.
Communicate about technology using appropriate terminology.	Design, develop, and present technology-based products for use inside and outside the classroom.	Exhibit ethical and legal behaviors when using information and technology.	Make informed choices about technology systems and resources.
Practice responsible use of technology and software.	Apply productivity tools to support personal and group productivity.	Use appropriate technology to accomplish a variety of tasks and to solve problems.	Use technology for managing and communicating personal and professional information.
Use technology for problem solving, communications, and idea sharing.	Use technology for research and inquiry.	Demonstrate an understanding of hardware, software, and networks.	Use technology for research, analysis, problem-solving, and decision making.

specific standards for their teachers. For example, the National Council of Teachers of English offers two technology-based standards in its recent Standards for English Language Arts (NCTE, 1996).

> Standard 7: Students conduct research on issues and interests by generating ideas and questions and by posing problems. They gather, evaluate, and synthesize data from a variety of sources to communicate their discoveries in ways that suit their purpose and audience.

> Standard 8: Students use a variety of technological and informational resources to gather and synthesize information and create and communicate knowledge.

The National Council of Teachers of Mathematics also has its Principles and Standards for School Mathematics, which states that "mathematics instructional programs should use technology to help all students understand mathematics and should prepare them to use mathematics in an increasingly technological world" (NCTM, 2000, p. 11).

Finally, the National Council of Social Studies adopted its curriculum standards in 1994 and included several thematic standards that use technology tools to support its learning goals for students in Pre-K to high school.

Teacher's task.   The teacher's task is to develop the evaluation instrument after considering the instructional requirements, resource materials, and technologies to be employed. Characteristics of good assessment include content that matches the teacher's lesson objectives and instructional emphasis, instruction that enhances student knowledge, clear and concise expectations for student performance, and minimum confounding factors. Assessment tools are typically characterized in three major categories: *Objective assessments* use multiple-choice, true-false, matching, and completion items. They measure the stages of learning from entry-level knowledge to its most complex stages. *Subjective assessments* are used to their best advantage when measuring higher-order mental processes such as application, analysis, and evaluation. Essay questions are perhaps the most well-known form of subjective assessments. *Authentic assessments* address problems of everyday life and include student investigations and showcase portfolios. Select objective, subjective, or authentic assessments, and revise the tool as necessary before use. An evaluation tool is provided in Appendix 11.1 to direct the assessment of technology-based materials.

STEP 9: SELECT THE INSTRUCTIONAL RESOURCES

The final step in lesson design is to select instructional materials.

Key characteristics.   The teacher must decide which technologies, if any, to use. There are a number of factors to consider before reaching a decision. For example, the technology must fit the age, experience, and knowledge level of the learner. It must be appropriate for the content being taught in terms of treatment, accuracy, and currency, and it should be closely related to the instructional purpose and learning objectives to be accomplished. The medium must communicate the necessary content, and the teacher must provide ample opportunity for students to engage in active, hands-on learning.

Teacher's task.   Technology-based instructional resources take the form of text-based student handouts, workbooks, and study guides; visual-based classroom presentations; and web-based course pages. Additionally, a few guidelines for selecting instructional resources are offered for consideration.

- No single category of instructional resource is best for all situations.
- Instructional resources should support learning objectives, not dictate them.
- Instructional resources must harmonize with the instructor's teaching style.
- Instructional resources must address student capabilities and learning strengths.
- Teachers must be thoroughly familiar with all instructional resources before using them in class.
- Instructional resources must be chosen objectively and not on the basis of personal preference.
- Instructional resources must be used in light of the physical environment of the classroom.

Section II completes the Technology Facade Checklist by examining learning outcomes. Question 20 requires an analysis of student responses to the technology experience. Because classroom computers and the computer lab are the most obvious environments for describing the learning experience, points are awarded for the appropriate use of this technology. However, this question should be asked only of students in grades 6 and above; allow the classroom teacher to respond for all other classes.

Section II: Technology Facade
Checklist Item 20

20. **How do students* in the computer classroom/laboratory describe their experience? Select one.**

	Points Available	Points Awarded
Play time or game time	0	
Unstructured, not sure of expected learning outcomes	1	
Applicable to what they are covering in class	5	
Appropriate for current classes and important for required/anticipated future skills	7	
Your Score (7 possible)	➡	

*This question restricted to students and their teachers in grades 6 and above.

ITEM 20—THE STUDENTS' EXPERIENCE

Purpose of the Question

The final question pertains to a subjective evaluation of how students use technology to learn. Unfortunately, any subjective assessment is necessarily biased; but a biased evaluation is better than none at all. To remove some of the inherent unfairness in such a question, item 20 is restricted to classrooms of grade 6 and above. By the time these students reach the age of 11 or 12, administrators and teachers should consider their students' opinions regarding their own learning. Most students can tell you whether there is intentional learning going on and whether the knowledge and skills in computer class are useful.

Justification for Points Awarded

Play time or game time (0 points).   A popular manifestation of the Technology Facade relates a story of students seemingly hard at work at the computer. On closer examination, they are found to be enjoying the latest arcade game or web site, neither of which has anything to do with their lesson. Children are very good at describing the benefits of their technology program; listen closely before awarding any points for this question.

Unstructured, not sure of expected learning outcomes (1 point).   Older students recognize an unstructured class—one without lesson goals or learning objectives. Even if students are using the latest educational software, only 1 point is appropriate if that software is not an integral part of the lesson.

Applicable to what they are covering in class (5 points).   If a teacher points to a specific learning objective in a lesson plan, 5 points are given toward the composite score. The technology does not need to fit perfectly, word for word, with the objective. But it must lend itself to an observable student behavior, the class materials provided, and the criteria for successful learning established by the teacher.

Appropriate for current classes and important for required/anticipated future skills (7 points).   An additional 2 points are available when technology is viewed as both a discipline and a tool. Today, technology is much more than just a tool for learning. Being technologically literate assumes a technology vocabulary (found in every grade-level standard from the ISTE) along with an understanding of its importance in today's workplace and the marketplace of tomorrow.

Issues to Consider When Assessing This Item

- Technology is the application of tools, materials, processes, and systems to solve problems. Technology involves a broad spectrum of knowledge and activities and combines knowledge of content, process, and skills to provide students with a holistic approach to learning.
- Organizations are stepping up to the challenge of educational standards in a major way. Every academic content area offers a set of standards for consideration during lesson development. A few of the very best standards for mathematics, science, performing arts, English, and social studies are shown in Table 11.2.
- Many states have defined standards for their content areas. Table 11.3 may be used to locate the standards specific to your particular state. Most states offer criteria for mathematics, science, performing arts, English, and social studies in addition to technology. If standards have not been developed in your area of concentration, consider using the work of another state.

Recommendations for Increasing the Points Awarded

1.   Review your state standards for teaching with technology, and discuss among faculty and administrators how these requirements can be converted into future classroom skills.

2.   Conduct an in-service teacher training session, and describe what technology competencies students should know and which technological skills students should possess at appropriate grade levels.

3.   Help your school provide students with a broad spectrum of technical activities while combining knowledge of content, process, and skills for a holistic approach to learning.

TABLE 11.2   **National Associations for Academic Standards**

WEB ADDRESS	ORGANIZATION	CONTENTS
www.enc.org	Eisenhower National Clearinghouse (ENC) Online	Standards from the National Council of Teachers of Mathematics and National Academy of Sciences
www.civiced.org/ curriculum.html	Center for Civic Education	Standards for civic education
http://artsedge. kennedy-center.org	Kennedy Center for the Performing Arts	Standards for the performing arts
www.nssb.org	The National Skill Standards Board (NSSB)	National system of skill standards, assessment, and certification systems to enhance the ability of the United States workforce to compete effectively in a global economy
www.mcrel.org/ compendium/ browse.asp	McREL, a private, nonprofit applied research and development organization	A compilation of content standards for K–12 curriculum
www.socialstudies. org/standards	National Council for Social Studies (NCSS)	NCSS published its Expectations of Excellence: Curriculum Standards for Social Studies
www.ncte.org/ standards	Sponsored by the National Council of Teachers of English (NCTE) and the International Reading Association (IRA)	Standards for English and the language arts

4. Consider technology in light of other content areas and as its own content area to be taught. As a minimum, integrate the following technology-related topics into the curriculum:

- Use of basic technology tools to solve problems
- Use of instruments and apparatus to study materials
- Application of basic computer operations and concepts
- Use of computer software to solve specific problems
- Identification of basic computer communications systems

TABLE 11.3   Web Addresses of the Departments of Education for All 50 States and the District of Columbia

Alabama	www.alsde.edu
Alaska	www.educ.state.ak.us
Arizona	www.ade.state.az.us
Arkansas	http://arkedu.state.ar.us
California	www.cde.ca.gov
Colorado	www.cde.state.co.us:80
Connecticut	www.state.ct.us/sde/
Delaware	http://doe.state.de.us
District of Columbia	www.k12.dc.us
Florida	www.firn.edu/doe
Georgia	www.doe.k12.ga.us
Hawaii	www.k12.hi.us
Idaho	www.sde.state.id.us
Illinois	www.isbe.state.il.us
Indiana	www.doe.state.in.us
Iowa	www.state.ia.us/educate
Kansas	www.ksbe.state.ks.us
Kentucky	www.kde.state.ky.us/otec
Louisiana	www.doe.state.la.us
Maine	http://janus.state.me.us/education
Maryland	www.msde.state.md.us
Massachusetts	www.doe.mass.edu
Michigan	www.mde.state.mi.us
Minnesota	www.educ.state.mn.us
Mississippi	www.mde.k12.ms.us
Missouri	http://dese.state.mo.us
Montana	www.metnet.state.mt.us
Nebraska	http://nde4.nde.state.ne.us
Nevada	www.nsn.k12.nv.us/nvdoe
New Hampshire	www.state.nh.us/doe
New Jersey	www.state.nj.us/education
New Mexico	http://sde.state.nm.us
New York	www.nysed.gov/
North Carolina	www.dpi.state.nc.us
North Dakota	www.dpi.nd.us

TABLE 11.3   Continued

Ohio	www.ode.state.oh.us
Oklahoma	http://sde.state.ok.us/
Oregon	www.ode.state.or.us
Pennsylvania	www.pde.psu.edu
Rhode Island	www.rid.oe.net
South Carolina	www.state.sc.us/sde
South Dakota	www.state.sd.us/state/executive/deca
Tennessee	www.state.tn.us/education
Texas	www.tea.state.tx.us
Utah	www.usoe.k12.ut.us
Vermont	www.state.vt.us/educ
Virginia	www.pen.k12.va.us/go/VDOE
Washington	www.k12.wa.us
West Virginia	http://wvde.state.wv.us
Wisconsin	www.dpi.state.wi.us
Wyoming	www.k12.wy.us

BIBLIOGRAPHY

ARTSEDGE, The John F. Kennedy Center for the Performing Arts.
    http://artsedge.kennedy-center.org
Center for Civic Education.
    www.civiced.org/curriculum.html
Eisenhower National Clearinghouse for Mathematics and Science Education, U.S. Department
    of Education, Office of Educational Research and Improvement (OERI).
    www.enc.org
International Society for Technology in Education. *National Educational Technology Standards
    for Students.* Eugene, OR: Author, 2000.
Kemp, Jerrold E., Ross, Steven M., and Morrison, Gary R. *Designing Effective Instruction,* 3rd ed.
    New York: John Wiley & Sons, 2000.
Mid-continent Research for Education and Learning (MREL).
    www.mcrel.org/compendium/browse.asp
National Skills Standards Board.
    www.nssb.org
National Council for the Social Studies.
    www.socialstudies.org/standards
National Council of Teachers of English. "Standards for the English Language Arts." 1996. Re-
    trieved June 5, 2000 from www.ncte.org/standards
National Council of Teachers of Mathematics. *Principles and Standards for School Mathematics.*
    Reston, VA: Author, 2000.

Appendix 11.1

Assessing Technology-Based Materials

Section I.
General Lesson Evaluation

1. Description of the Lesson

_____

_____

_____

2. Lesson objectives (specify)
   a.

_____

_____

Enter Rating Here ➡

   b.

_____

_____

Enter Rating Here ➡

   c.

_____

_____

Enter Rating Here ➡

   d.

_____

_____

Enter Rating Here ➡

3. Critique of lesson success

_____

_____

_____

Enter Rating Here ➡

Section II. Technologies Evaluation

Rate each item from 1 (poor use of technology) to 5 (excellent use of technology).
Enter "N/U" if technology was not used during the lesson.

Classroom Computers	Lab Computers	Education Software	Audio-visual	Other

Section III. Materials Evaluation

Rate each item from 1 (poor use of technology) to 5 (excellent use of technology).
Enter "N/U" if technology was not used during the lesson.

Materials consistent with curriculum objectives					
Materials consistent with individual lesson objectives					
Content of materials appropriate for the lesson/students					
Content of materials appropriately sequenced					
Materials used in logical sequence					
Content of materials up-to-date					
Content of materials accurately reflects current thinking					
Materials capture student interest					
Materials appropriate for learner's abilities					
Materials adaptable to variety of learning situations					
Materials free from cultural bias					
Overall quality of the materials					
Materials justify their costs					
Materials appropriate for time allowed					

Section IV. Evaluation Average Score

Section I of this assessment tool provides for general lesson evaluation and describes the lesson along with its applicable objectives. Listing the indicative data for the lesson focuses the teacher's attention on the important elements that are to be assessed. Enter a brief description of the lesson in item 1. Enter up to four lesson objectives in item 2 (additional objectives can be listed at the bottom of the tool). Finally, enter a short critique of the lesson—was it successful?

Section II rates the lesson's technologies. A Likert scale from 1 (poor use of technology) to 5 (excellent use of technology) provides for the assessment of the major technologies heading each column. A blank column is available to specify other technologies. To the right of each lesson objective, rate each technology used during the lesson. Enter "N/U" if no technology was necessary to complete this objective.

Section III evaluates instructional materials: text-, visual-, and web-based. The same Likert rating scale used in Section II assigns a value to each of these criteria. Remember, this section deals specifically with instructional materials used in the lesson.

Section IV completes the evaluation tool by averaging the scores for each of the technologies evaluated. Add the scores and divide by the number of entries. Although they are not a statistical measure of success, these numbers will provide some measure of comparison for future lessons.

PART V

EPILOGUE

> *The Technology Facade: "The use of technology in a school or school district without benefit of the necessary infrastructure to adequately support its use as a viable instructional strategy."*

Defining the Technology Facade set the stage for a thorough examination of the many ways in which schools overcome barriers to effective instructional technology in the classroom—barriers that continue to sap their declining budgets and reduced personnel resources. It is projected that over $600 billion will be spent on education during each of the first several years of the new millennium. If history is any indicator, that number will undoubtedly continue to rise throughout the first decade of the 2000s.

Since 1978, with the introduction of the first commercial personal computer, technology has consumed its fair share of a school's limited resources, and many expect this percentage to increase. Eliminating as many of the identified shortfalls of a technology program is only good stewardship of the taxpayer's money. Fortunately, there is now an instrument for measuring the health of a technology program that is based on research and comprehensive in scope.

Regardless of the final composite score achieved by a school during the initial application of the Technology Facade Checklist, the issues and recommendations presented in these chapters will make technology programs stronger and ensure that computers, software, and networks become a strategy of choice for classroom teaching and learning.

ISSUES FOR SCHOOLS, TEACHERS, AND STUDENTS

Schools find themselves to be both producers and consumers on the information superhighway. Federal programs contribute in large measure to a multibillion-dollar-a-year telecommunications budget just to keep our classrooms connected. Whether those programs will continue to provide such funds has all the makings of an administrator's nightmare. Schools are looking to web technology as a platform for advertising their programs and communicating with their clients. Technology must remain reliable; without the necessary funding, its future as an administrative tool is in doubt.

Increasingly, teachers find themselves on the uphill side of what seems like a perpetual learning curve. Just when they have become comfortable with their academic content areas, technology rapidly sneaks up on them. Only a few years ago, teachers could avoid technology if they chose to do so. Sure, their students were using computers at home and spending valuable class time discussing the latest in handheld video games. But the effect of technology in the classroom appeared minimal or, at the very least, controllable. Then came the explosion of the World Wide Web, megahertz-speed processors, multimedia software, and the megabit-per-second communications that made it all possible. Suddenly, education changed. Schools are now spending millions of dollars on computers and software. However, only 9 percent of their technology budgets go toward teacher preparation. Computers are viewed as tools for the lab rather than the classroom, and what limited preparation teachers do receive is still in the form of skills and competencies instead of curriculum application.

Students want to know how to research the history of the American Revolution using CD-ROM–based encyclopedias. They need help in computer class with their spreadsheets and what-if scenarios. They do not understand why a cut-and-paste version of a book report constitutes plagiarism and causes such violent teacher reaction. High school seniors are in a desperate struggle to ready themselves for a climate they already know demands more skills than they now possess. Statistics show that over 70 percent of graduating seniors use technology routinely, leaving the other 30 percent who arrive for their first college semester already at a significant disadvantage. Technology standards have been approved and implemented in 32 states, but what about the other 18 states? How can those students compete in the workplace or classroom of the future?

BARRIERS TO AN EFFECTIVE TECHNOLOGY PROGRAM

The Technology Facade exists today in most schools. Few have advanced to the state of the art that justifies an A rating from the Checklist. The demands of technology on dwindling resources makes it imperative that schools acknowledge the existence of the Technology Facade, understand its impact on resources and budgets, and seek to defeat or at least moderate its effects on the teacher in the classroom. This book suggests numerous strategies for action.

The Technology Facade contains three elements—the use of technology, the necessary infrastructure, and a viable instructional strategy. Understanding the essential components of a successful technology program is the first step in overcoming the Facade. The Technology Facade Checklist is an objective tool for assessing the school's current status of hardware and software, the inherent weaknesses of its foundation, and the deep-seated reluctance to integrate technology into the curriculum. For many schools, the final composite score is a rude awakening, perhaps even a serious bruise to the reputation of the administrators, faculty, and staff. But this short-term affront must be quickly replaced with a renewed commitment to resolve every deficiency identified in the Checklist.

THE CHALLENGES OF
THE TECHNOLOGY FACADE

After reading this book, applying the Checklist, and analyzing the results, schools should embark on a plan. They have been given all the necessary components for a new strategy. They can set their courses with a compass to ensure their arrival at the final destination. Schools can do no less for their teachers and their students. The time has come to make a total commitment to *use technology in a school or school district* with *the benefit of the necessary infrastructure to adequately support its use as a viable instructional strategy.*

CHAPTER 12

REFLECTING ON THE
TECHNOLOGY FACADE

Part One, Introducing the Technology Facade, offered a scheme for recognizing the Technology Facade by developing a working definition of its components, applying a rubric to evaluate its effects, and analyzing and assessing its impact on a school.

Chapter 1, Defining the Technology Facade, presented the reader with a description of the three elements that comprise the phenomenon. "The use of technology in a school or school district" distinguished among the terms *technology, educational technology,* and *instructional technology.* The discussion concentrated on instructional technology and the many uses of technology in the classroom for teaching and learning. "The necessary infrastructure to support its use" established the new "three M's" of instructional technology—an axiom for men, money, and materials that transposes into people, funding, and resources. Finally, "a viable instructional strategy" considered the preparation of instructional lessons using technology and the integration of these resources into the curriculum. A model for preparing technology-based lessons provided teachers with this newest strategy for designing an environment of multisensory learning.

Chapter 2 is the heart of the book. Created as a pull-out section for easy application, this chapter contains the entire Technology Facade Checklist, the eight-step process for its application, and the Checklist Analysis and Composite Score Forms.

Now that you've read about the Checklist, you can take the following steps to implement it: Distribute the Checklist to all schools in the region to produce a districtwide analysis of technology for the school board. Consider each question during upcoming in-service training sessions. Create a virtual score card for tracking program improvements and addressing key weaknesses throughout the academic year. Use the results to encourage more active participation among the people of the Technology Facade. Refrain from pointing fingers and futile accusations; try not to compare one school's scores against another. There is enough of that going on already with test scores and national classroom trends. Modify the individual questions, the responses, and even the points to reflect how the school operates, students learn, and teachers teach.

Obtain the permission of administrators before conducting the Checklist. Schedule an appointment with the technology coordinator. Validate the results to ensure they are consistent. Finally, present the results to decision makers and begin a continuous improvement program to address the identified weaknesses of the program.

Part Two, The Use of Technology, continued the scheme for decreasing the effects of the Technology Facade and increasing the composite score, by concentrating on the uses of available technologies for the classroom, defining the computer competencies and skills required for teachers and students, and classifying technologies according to their ability to communicate and teach.

Chapter 3 introduced the reader to the first of three critical components of the use of technology, which represent 55 of the possible 200 points on the Checklist. To decrease the effects of the Technology Facade, the use of technology must include an understanding of the technologies found in today's classroom along with the computer competencies and skills required of teachers and students. The chapter discusses new technologies at the teacher's disposal, along with recommendations on how to model, demonstrate, and apply them in the classroom. The chapter presented hardware, software, and network items—from calculators to word processing. Checklist Items 1, 2, and 3 award points for the scope of technology use by teachers, access to technology within the school plant, and placement of computers throughout the school plant. The discussion centered around the importance of integrating technology into every teacher's classroom, permitting all-day access to technology, and integrating technology into the library, computer lab, and all classrooms.

Chapter 4 established a set of technical competencies and skills for teachers and students. The International Society for Technology in Education (ISTE) offers a series of competencies for teacher candidates seeking initial certification. The competencies included basic computer terminology, personal and professional use of technology, and practical applications of technology in instruction. The National Council for Accreditation of Teacher Education has proposed a new set of student technology skills, including the identification of computer parts and vocabulary, use and care of technology, and use of software applications, including multimedia and presentation applications. This chapter discussed each of these competencies and skills in detail and tendered a logical progression of these abilities from introduction to practice to mastery to application. Checklist items 4 and 5 rated a teacher's use of technology for grading, lesson preparation, homework assignments, and in-class presentations. Scoring the use of student learning objectives in technology-based lesson plans was also addressed.

Chapter 5 discussed the uses of classroom technology and examined a taxonomy of instructional technology, proposed for the first time in this book. This chapter focused on the use of technology for communications, instruction, decision making, and technical literacy, plus it offered a look at how technology affects society. Checklist item 6 rated a school's educational software, its currency and potential for meeting curriculum objectives, and how these tools are selected.

Part Three, The Necessary Infrastructure, examined the infrastructure of a school's technology program; specifically, its people, funding, and resources. Chapter 6 introduced the many cast members of the Technology Facade and presented each key player in the best possible light. The contributions of students, teachers, curriculum designers, technology coordinators, the business manager, parents, community and corporate leaders, school board members, the various departments of education, the principal, and technology committee members were considered. Checklist items 7, 8, 9, and 10 explore the people of the Facade and assign points for their involvement in the technology program. The extent of teachers' training and their participation on a school's technology committee raises important concerns. The issue of committee participation is expanded in subsequent questions to include other key individuals. Finally, technology professionals are scored and schools are awarded points for hiring technology coordinators, administrators, technicians, and teachers. Appendixes 6.1 and 6.2 present a draft in-service training agenda for teachers and a recommended program of study for formal training in instructional technology.

Chapter 7 dealt with the question of funding a technology program. The costs are growing as schools vie to remain current with the latest in computers, Internet connectivity, and educational software. It is not an enviable position for administrators, who often measure their school's status by the number and age of the computers in their labs. To avoid the Facade-stricken condition of funding technology only with monies remaining at the end of the academic year, a school chart of accounts was proposed with classifications, accounts, and budget codes that work in any school situation. Checklist items 11 and 12 gauge how successfully a program is budgeted. Several options are awarded points, but only a technology program with its own specific, recurring line item in the annual budget merits the full points. A separate funding issue concerns itself with compensating teachers who pursue excellence in instructional technology. A formal awards programs is acceptable in the short run; however, only a program that offers monetary remuneration receives full credit.

The resources identified in Chapter 8 presented a wide range of factors that make for a successful technology program. Nothing, however, is more important than a school's technology plan. An effective plan contains the ingredients addressed in this chapter: hardware, software, network, instruction, community relations, assessment, and fiscal and facility planning. Online copyright issues and the laws associated with the fair use of electronic works were presented in Appendix 8.1. Checklist items 13, 14, and 15 explore the strengths and weaknesses of the school's technology plan. Question 13 looks for the existence of a plan and its currency, whereas question 14 awards points for each important component of a viable plan. Question 15 assesses the school's computers with points for machines that are newer, multimedia-equipped, and connected to both printers and the Internet.

Part Four, A Viable Instructional Strategy, discussed the instructional component of this book: Planning the curriculum, planning the integration of technologies into lessons, and planning for successful learning. Part Four provided a roadmap of nine steps for victory over the Technology Facade.

Moving into a discussion of the viable instructional strategy, Chapter 9 looked at planning the curriculum and how technology is impacted by the instructional design process. The Kemp model offered a nine-step paradigm for designing a technology-based lesson. This chapter examined the first five steps to define the problem, describe learner characteristics, identify the subject content, state the instructional objectives, and sequence the content of the lesson. Appendix 9.1 presented a detailed scope and sequence for teaching technology from kindergarten through high school. Checklist items 16 and 17 determine whether a school's scope and sequence address student technology competencies; if so, points are awarded for specificity and comprehensiveness. The chapter discussed how behavioral, cognitive, and humanistic psychology produce successful technology-based learning objectives. Teachers gain considerable insight into how technology affects the related teaching styles of mastery learning, discovery learning, reception learning, open education, and cooperative learning.

Chapter 10 centered on the instructional systems design model, Steps 6 and 7. In Step 6, the reader was given the key characteristics and teacher's tasks for designing the instructional strategies and resource materials. Step 7 offered the selection of technologies from among computers, video, audio, multimedia, and more. An extremely important section of the book, this chapter provided a text-based workbook, visual-based classroom presentation, and web-based lesson to serve as a guide to developing teacher-made, technology-based materials. Checklist items 18 and 19 examine these materials to determine whether teachers have actually integrated these personalized resources into their curricula. The follow-on question describes what typically happens when a teacher tries to use technology: are the technologies open and readily accessible, or characteristically unavailable?

Chapter 11 completed the scrutiny of a school's technology program with a plan for successful learning that included developing evaluation instruments and choosing the instructional resources for the lesson. The evaluation guide in Appendix 11.1, Assessing Technology-Based Materials, helps teachers assess the uses of classroom technology for student learning. The final Checklist item, question 20, changes the pace of previous evaluations by asking students to describe their learning experiences with technology.

RETHINKING THE TECHNOLOGY FACADE SCENARIOS

Part One considered a collection of scenarios and invited readers to check off whether these descriptions could be found in their own schools. Each scenario indicated a different manner in which the Technology Facade is evidenced in schools. After assessing the technology program and implementing the recommended strategies offered in Chapters 3 through 11, readers are able to address the deficiencies in their technology programs, increase the total composite scores on the Checklist, and reduce the impact of the Technology Facade. Following are some new scenarios that depict the successful school.

☑ SCENARIO CHECKLIST

Our computer lab sports the latest processors, the fastest CD-ROM players, the largest memory capacities, and the most sophisticated multimedia sound systems. Teachers clamor to use the technologies identified in Chapter 3. Most would prefer computers in the classroom, but they understand their school budget and work around the funding limits of the current program. They are confident that our program will only get better.

☐ You will find this scenario in my school.

☐ This scenario does not describe my school.

Our state-of-the-art computer lab is filled with Macintosh or Windows personal computers. However, teachers still find it difficult to secure a machine for themselves because students are in the labs during study halls, before school, and after school. The situation is tolerable and even desirable as both teachers and students strive to master the skills and competencies identified in Chapter 4. There are no locks on the labs during the day, they are staffed with volunteers supported by professional technologists, and a help desk is available (sometimes manned with students from the computer science club) to help with questions and hardware problems.

☐ You will find this scenario in my school.

☐ This scenario does not describe my school.

The principal tours our middle school with the parents of next year's prospective batch of incoming sixth graders, promoting Mrs. Schnieder's three-day-a-week computer classes for all students. When a parent asks about the computer lab, they are shown the latest, state-of-the-art technology, software that is available in local computer stores, and excited teachers and students who praise the efforts of everyone who has made the computer lab possible. Many students still boast better computer setups at home. However, the principal understands Chapter 5 and the taxonomy of instructional technology and is able to satisfactorily explain to parents that the real question to consider is not, "Do we have the latest and greatest technology money can buy?," but, "Can the technology we have in our labs and classroom teach our children the computer skills they need to succeed?" And our answer is a resounding "Yes!"

☐ You will find this scenario in my school.

☐ This scenario does not describe my school.

Our school has the most up-to-date technology available. There is not another school in our district that compares to our computers, network, or educational software library. All teachers and staff members attended their initial in-service training session less than 6 months ago and continue to participate in at least four technology in-service training sessions each year, on topics recommended in Chapter 6. Many students still understand more about these tools than the teachers do, but teachers have integrated the technology into their curricula and expect students to use technology to learn.

☐ You will find this scenario in my school.

☐ This scenario does not describe my school.

Our school handbook contains a technology section describing hardware and software available to the community—students, parents, local organizations, and individual citizens. After nearly 2 years of bake sales, candy drives, and magazine campaigns, the technology program is now funded by an annual recurring operating budget recommended in Chapter 7. The new budget, approved and supported by our principal, ensures that planned replacements and upgrades are scheduled, and, should year-end funds become available, the money will be distributed fairly among "regular" academic programs, including technology.

☐ You will find this scenario in my school.

☐ This scenario does not describe my school.

Our school's technology plan is scheduled to be updated during the last 3 months of the school year. The plan contains most, if not all, of the elements recommended in Chapter 8 and is considered a "living document" by all members of the Technology Committee.

☐ You will find this scenario in my school.

☐ This scenario does not describe my school.

Teachers applaud recent changes to school policy regarding access to the school's computer lab for special in-class projects. We applied the recommended scope and sequence from Chapter 9 and found plenty of time available for those projects that require Internet support or extra hands-on computer time.

☐ You will find this scenario in my school.

☐ This scenario does not describe my school.

Teachers, not the technology coordinator, brief dignitaries on the benefits of computers to our school. They talk about how computers are used in academic content areas such as math, science, social studies, and language arts. The teachers show visiting parents the text-, visual-, and web-based resources they have developed using Chapter 10 as a guide. Each parent is offered a brochure of upcoming training sessions, especially for those who want to understand how technology is being used in the classroom. Parents, community leaders, and alumni are actively solicited as potential members of the school's Technology Committee; some even volunteer for team work.

☐ You will find this scenario in my school.

☐ This scenario does not describe my school.

Parents were informed about the technology skills expected of their first graders and how these were rationally a smaller sub-set of fifth-grade or eighth-grade competencies. They were able to understand that 2 hours of computers every week was sufficient to master the skill set expected for the earlier grades, leaving extra time for the larger skill set required of graduating students. All students are prepared for the technical challenges of the next level and give our technology program "two thumbs up" against the criteria established in Chapter 11.

☐ You will find this scenario in my school.

☐ This scenario does not describe my school.

Student–teacher classroom ratios continue to decline, while certification demands on overtaxed teachers grow with the passage of nearly every new educational bill. Three-quarters or more of public and private students are taught technology skills by teachers not certified as instructional technologists. Many states do not even have a certification program for preparing instructional technology classroom teachers. Science and math teachers are plucked from their classrooms, sometimes voluntarily, other times under duress, to teach a growing litany of computer skills and competencies to high school and college-bound graduates.

Teachers are known to possess literacy skills in the language arts similar to (or exceeding) private-sector executives and managers, engineers, physicians, writers and artists, social workers, sales representatives, education administrators, and registered nurses. But nearly 60 percent of fourth graders reported that they never use computers in their mathematics class and another 70 percent of eighth graders report the same thing (Orlofsky and Jerald, 1999).

Even if well-trained, 7 out of 10 teachers say they have difficulty finding software that would make the classroom computers valuable (Orlofsky and Jerald, 1999).

There is no scarcity of educational software, but much of it is not useful or does not help teachers in their quest to give students the information they need to do well on standardized tests. Searching for the right software takes up more time than most teachers have, and only a few states have created a software clearinghouse that preselects software for how well it helps students meet educational standards. There is much less software for junior high and high school students than for elementary students, despite the fact that studies show that older students may benefit even more from computer learning than younger students do.

Still, a lot of money is being spent for software. In 1999, schools spent $340 million on stand-alone software and $218 million for comprehensive courseware. Another $13 million was spent on online subscriptions because some teachers prefer to use web sites on the Internet to supplement their curricula (Quality Education Data, 2000).

National marketing surveys present a similar picture when it comes to access to home computers. Nationally, in 1997, the U.S. Census Bureau reported that 36.6 percent of the U.S. population (37.4 million Americans) owned a home computer, and nearly half (49.7 percent) of school-age children routinely use home computers for entertainment, personal development, or as part of their homework assignments. Teachers fall miserably below these national norms. Less than 1 in 20 classroom teachers owns a home computer, and 86 percent have had less than 20 hours of training on basic technology skills in the last 12 months (U.S. Census Bureau, 1997).

The Technology Facade is alive and well. But for those interested in reducing its effects and enhancing their technology programs, the recommendations and strategies found in this book will be invaluable.

BIBLIOGRAPHY

Quality Education Data, Inc. "Ten Trends to Watch in Instructional Technology." 2000. Retrieved July 22, 2000 from www.qeddata.com

Orlofsky, Greg F., and Jerald, Craig D. "Raising the Bar on School Technology," *Education Week,* September 23, 1999.

U.S. Census Bureau. *Home Ownership of Computers, By Population Classification.* Washington, DC: U.S. Government Printing Office, 1997.

INDEX